Edubabble

A GLOSSARY OF TEACHER TALK

CLYDE WOOLMAN

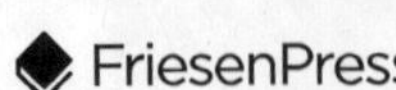

Suite 300 - 990 Fort St
Victoria, BC, V8V 3K2
Canada

www.friesenpress.com

First Edition — 2018

ISBN
978-1-5255-2588-9 (Hardcover)
978-1-5255-2589-6 (Paperback)
978-1-5255-2590-2 (eBook)

1. *Humor, Topic, School & Education*

Distributed to the trade by The Ingram Book Company

ABOUT THE AUTHOR

Clyde Woolman has been a teacher and counselor, a principal of an elementary, a middle and three high schools; and completed a six-year hiatus as a Superintendent (CEO) of a school district before reengaged neurons led him to voluntarily announce a return to a school. At one time or another he has been involved in education from Kindergarten through to the university level. He has delivered keynote speeches at conferences, sat on panels, presented workshops and seminars, and led teacher and principal teams when reporting on schools. Instead of incessantly talking about the trials and tribulations of teachers and schools, he decided to compile this glossary as a tribute to those adults working and supporting the students in their care.

Also written for teachers is *Hepting's Road: A Novel of Teaching* (FriesenPress 2018). Woolman has also published two adventure novels for children 10-12 years old, released by Moosehide Books: *Yurek: Edge of Extinction* (2013), and *Smugglers at the Lighthouse* (2010).

Go to www.clydewoolman.com for more information.

TO ALL THE TEACHERS IN PUBLIC EDUCATION;

MAY YOU KEEP ON DOING THE GOOD THAT YOU DO,

AND KEEP YOUR SENSE OF HUMOR WHEN DOING IT.

ACKNOWLEDGMENTS

Thanks to Dave Brooker, who is as fine an editor as he was a teacher, and to the teachers and administrators with whom I have shared so many of the stories that led to this project. You know who you are.

Special appreciation is extended to my loving wife, life partner and fellow teacher, Ileana Woolman.

PREFACE

In over thirty years as a teacher, counselor, principal of elementary, middle and high schools, as well as six years as superintendent of schools (a CEO position in the jurisdiction in which I worked), I heard and witnessed much humor in remarks and action. Many teachers and principals believed that a manuscript commenting on the quirks and foibles of the teacher workplace would be an enjoyable read. “Someone should write this stuff down,” was an oft-repeated phrase. This was usually in response one of three occurrences; the verbiage or antics of children or teens, the perplexing decisions made by education bureaucrats (including those made by myself), or the fatuous statements emanating from professors and/or politicians trumpeting the need for systemic change in public education.

It also occurred to me that teachers speak a common language dotted with acronyms and jargon few in the profession probe for real meaning. Educators share a common organizational culture, created not only by the realities of their workplace, but by the thoughts and statements of non-teachers both powerful and proletarian, who are rarely shy about voicing opinion. This shared culture and language is found at all levels; elementary, middle, and high school; in buildings large and small; in settings rural, suburban, and urban core. The enrolment area may be affluent or economically challenged; the teachers well paid, (good luck with that one) or struggling with meager paychecks.

So, one day, when a teacher issued a seemingly offhand remark that, "No one will ever believe this stuff, someone should write it down," the impetus for a two-pronged "literary" approach was launched. The result was the novel *Hepting's Road,* and this humor compilation, *Edubabble: A Glossary of Teacher Talk*. They are quite dissimilar, not the least difference being that the former is a novel and this glossary is a brief compilation of education-oriented humor.

While there are always exceptions to any rule, I have found the vast majority of teachers to be dedicated, many to the point of being altruistic. They possess high levels of intrinsic motivation and may be broadly described as individually conservative and collectively liberal. They appear to eschew flamboyant attire, often sporting forgettable, almost dull, fashion. They seem to prefer practical rather than flashy cars. These are generalizations to be sure, but there is enough fodder in these idiosyncratic character traits to form a thematic thread throughout the glossary.

A second overarching topic is the school as a unique employment venue. From supervision duty to the tyranny of the bell, and from lesson preparation to marking student work, there is much to say about how schools differ from most workplaces. Of course, the most obvious distinction is that they are populated by students; and what children and teenagers say and do can make for some entertaining descriptions. Several entries attempt to capture such shenanigans and comprise a third thematic thrust throughout the glossary.

A fourth leitmotif focuses on so-called "experts", who are forever telling teachers what to do and how to do it. While these people range from politicians to bureaucrats, and professors to self-proclaimed visionaries, the one trait they share is that they have rarely, if ever, worked in a school or taught in a classroom. Why some teachers pay so much attention to these people has always been a mystery to me.

I do not know why teaching is so prone to jargon, nor do I know why there are so many acronyms in education. I only know that much of the argot can only be described as nonsensical. Perhaps jargon and acronyms enhance understanding, though they seem more likely to contribute to further obfuscation. The continuing trend toward more edubabble is such a promising field that it made for an encapsulating title.

The themes are wrapped with intended humor. Of course, what constitutes humor depends upon the perception of the receiver, not the teller. As an educator, I am not a comedian. I do not tell jokes well and have never regarded myself as wryly sarcastic. I have tried to insert what I believe to be at least a dose of dry wit in most of the entries. There are comments offered for over three hundred terms or phrases and I hope people will find at least a few describe a truth hidden within the humor. I am sure some readers will groan at what they believe to be poor comedic satire expressed in some of the listings. Others may manage only a mild snicker at a comment or two. Some may be insulted by a few descriptions which may hit "too close to home."

A teaching career is a wonderful yet challenging expedition that is full of adventure. A little edubabble humor can help navigate the more difficult terrain and make the journey that is teaching all the more enjoyable.

Good luck and good reading.

A

A (LETTER GRADE) Bombarded by a media onslaught that promotes prosaic entertainment, forgettable fashion, and rampant consumerism, it is not surprising that students believe their own hype and that the mediocre work they produce deserves an outstanding review. When the middling quality of an assignment does not receive an A letter grade, it must be that the teacher has failed to grasp the brilliance of the work; *see Advertising, Grade Inflation, Helicopter Parents, Honor Roll.*

ABACUS An environmentally friendly power-free tool for calculating student marks, this device has a much longer track record than computers. It will not send data from a teacher's long hours of assessment into cyberspace, never to be seen again. This tool is cutting edge technology and highly recommended; *see Report Cards, Techno-Geek.*

ABBREVIATIONS LD (Learning Disabled), students frequently receive assistance from the LAT (Learning Assistance Teacher), who will develop an IEP (Individualized Education Plan), which should link with the student-driven ILP (Individual Learning Plan). MID (Moderate Intellectually Disabled), ADD (Attention Deficit Disorder), and ESL (English as a Second Language), students may also require extra assistance to meet the ILOs (Intended Learning Outcomes), as outlined by the government. The only conclusion from this "information" is that abbreviations add considerable weight to the mystique of edubabble; *see Edubabble, Learning Assistance Teacher, Psychobabble, Syndrome.*

ACADEMY In an era of marketing hype there is inherent value in a pretentious name that offers a hint of snobbery. Why name an institution Mountain View Arts School when Alpine Vista Fine Arts Academy, is available? The "academy" or "collegiate" title is thrown about in education almost as loosely as "resort" is for trailer parks, and "spa" for nail salons housed in shopping malls; *see Marketing, Names for Schools.*

ACCOUNTABILITY This financial term, with origins in ledgers and accounts, is enthusiastically applied by non-teachers to the complexities of human learning and the difficulties inherent in attempting to educate every citizen; *see Benchmarking, Data-Driven Decision Making, Diving Into the Data, Number Crunchers, Politicians, Voucher System.*

ADLERIAN INFERIORITY Any teacher who has taught two or more children from the same family will have views about birth order which may or may not jive with those of Alfred Adler. Unlike Adler, the teacher will not be a famous psychologist that has a philosophical break with Sigmund Freud or a spouse who is pals with Leon Trotsky. Such unabashed name-dropping of the famous and powerful may cause the teacher to believe that his or her opinion on birth order based on classroom experience is not worthy. Adler had much to say about an inferiority complex, and such teacher reticence would add credence to his theories.

ADVERTISING Only in high schools would one find a target audience comprising over three million impressionable teens who are captive in rooms with acres of empty wall space. The building could be crammed with poster sized ads for sugary soda, movie openings, and scantily-clad rock and rap stars. The potential for billboard profit is enormous. Teachers too, could receive much-needed cash with strategically placed ads on briefcases and desks; *see Apple Inc. (2), Back-to-School Sales, Budget, Zero (2).*

AIDES The title of these positions varies and can include teacher aide, education aide, paraprofessional, and special education aide. The quality of performance matches the titular variance and broadly comprises two typologies, the first thankfully much more prevalent than the second:

a) aides that, despite poor pay, meet or exceed the dedication and competence of the teachers with whom they work and are extremely helpful to the student(s) in their care. Many of these aides should have become teachers, principals, or superintendents; *see Altruism, Pay Slip (2), Self-Esteem (Teacher), Teacher, Undaunted;*

b) a tiny minority of aides whose presence is little more than a nuisance to the teacher, as if a bigger, older child has been registered in the class. These aides alternate between yakking incessantly about every nuance of the child's behavior each day and waiting for specific direction prior to initiating any work. Teacher attempts to include these adults in the class size count has not met with success, yet; *see Learned Helplessness, Tattlers and Squealers, Yarn.*

ALTRUISM Why would anyone with a university degree work for relatively low pay and receive such a minimum level of respect? The answer is that this attribute is an ingrained personality trait of many teachers; *see Aides (a), Kindergarten Teacher, Pay Slip (2), Teachers' High, Umpire (Professional Baseball), Undaunted, Zealot.*

AMANUENSIS One of the benefits of this glossary is to improve one's edubabble skills. An amanuensis is a person who takes dictation for another who is afflicted by the physical inability to write. Now the reader can throw the term amanuensis around the staffroom while others are left to use the far more proletarian expression, scribe.

APPLE INC.

1. Proving that any enterprise can be resurrected after falling far out of favor, people often forget that this now-dominant company was virtually defunct at the turn of the century. This demonstrates that even an underfunded, frequently unloved enterprise such as public education can make a startling comeback; *see Fidget, I Generation, Zeitgeist.*
2. Through adept advertising and marketing, the small but noticeable Apple logo is displayed on hundreds of thousands of computers across North American schools, making daily contact with the eyeballs of millions of students. It is always good marketing strategy to "condition" the consumer while he or she is young, and to do so in as covert a manner as possible; *see Advertising.*

APPLES Elementary school teachers appreciate receiving this traditional gift from students. High school teachers greet such a gesture with apprehension, checking first for unnatural additives and additions and then, when nobody is looking, pitching it into the nearest trash can; *see Fruit Flies.*

ART In an increasingly monitor-dominated world of visual excess, it is surprising that this subject, devoted at least in part to visual literacy, remains a frill for many decision makers in education; *see Frills, Murals, Relevance, Van Gogh.*

ASSEMBLY Like a semi-organized communal festival, this gathering brings the entire school together. Elementary students like to fidget and squirm, rarely paying attention to what is happening at the front of the gym. High school students like to fidget and squirm too, though they prefer to do so while poking and pawing at members of the opposite gender; *see Fidget, Jamming and Cramming.*

ASSESSMENT FOR LEARNING / ASSESSMENT OF LEARNING Understanding the difference between these two concepts is not a particularly challenging intellectual exercise. Yet the distinction is the subject of articles, conferences, and even books. Given that teachers are hardly dim-witted, the only logical explanation for the amount of verbiage is that education researchers have very little to talk or write about. The need to fill space on a page or air time at a conference is paramount. The long fluffy explanations, which are little more than common sense, are classic examples of edubabble; *see Authentic Assessment, Edubabble, Education Professors, Innovation.*

ATLAS Despite the prevalence of Google maps, students still like thumbing through an old-fashioned print atlas.

This may generate unwelcome questions from fourth or fifth grade children about geographic facts and concepts. The teacher may be unable to respond adequately; either due to the challenge of explaining a difficult concept or lack of knowledge. When employing the "sage on the stage" instructional style, one simply cannot know everything. If a question arises for which the answer is unknown, it is best to avoid the urge to concoct a falsehood. The world has enough fake news. A sampling of children's questions is:

a) "Since water flows downhill, why does the Nile River flow upward on the map?"
b) "If continents are larger than countries, why is Russia bigger than Antarctica?"
c) "Why is Kansas City in Missouri and not in Kansas?"
d) "Why is the Caspian Sea a sea when it is land-locked and should be called a lake?"
e) "If people in Hawaii and Puerto Rico are citizens of the United States, why is Hawaii a state and Puerto Rico isn't?"
f) "Where is the line that marks the end of the Gulf of Mexico and the beginning of the Caribbean Sea?"

see Infinity, Intelligence Level, Mercator Projection.

ATTENDANCE AT SCHOOL

1. A tiny minority of high school students believe that attending one class per week is legitimate grounds for remaining registered in the school.
2. A minority of central office bureaucrats believe that visiting the school once per year is legitimate evidence that they are "staying in touch."

AUTHENTIC ASSESSMENT A good example of edubabble, this term is an example of fluffy nothingness while sounding important, serious, and almost clinical. Before it was "authentic," was the assessment utilized pretend, fake, or phony? *see Learning Assistance Teacher, Professional Learning Community.*

B

BABY BOOM TEACHERS Just when younger teachers were enjoying the declining influence of baby boomers in education, a failed fad from the boomer years, open area classrooms, has shown signs of making a comeback. Can't the boomer generation just go away? *see I Generation, Innovation, Open Area Classrooms/Open Concept School, Veteran Teachers.*

BACKBONE Teachers should be careful about the traits they desire in a school leader. Some may advocate for a flexible, laissez-faire principal, only to find him or her to be as spineless as a jelly fish, changing course with every tiny shift in the tidal currents of education. Others may lobby for a principal with "backbone", only to find the individual to be as flexible as granite. A leader who has both attributes and can display each at the appropriate time is the ultimate win. Unfortunately, rock-hard jelly fish are truly freaks of nature and thus extremely rare; *see Principal (a-f).*

BACK-TO-SCHOOL SALES A prime example of business firms capitalizing on an educational event, this consumer frenzy has considerable potential for cash-strapped schools and their teachers. Wary of charges of commercialism, schools have been slow to take financial advantage, though the anticipated windfall could alleviate at least some of the inevitable budgetary challenges. As a bonus, teachers could act as spokespeople in commercials for the tools of the trade such as whiteboard markers, red pens, binders, and aspirin. The additional income would be welcomed and at least as ethical as kickbacks in the pharmaceutical industry.

In a previous era, the sales began in mid-August. Though the length of the summer break has remained constant, the blazing advertisements and promotional displays are now often seen about four days after the school year ends in the spring; *see Advertising, Budget, Dress, Jocks and Jockettes.*

BASKETBALL For reasons unknown, basketball seems to stimulate questionable coaching behavior. When the high school coach gapes in disbelief at the referee's poor eyesight; prays to the heavens as a bench warmer approaches the foul line; windmills frantic arms as if the breeze created can help team members run faster; kicks the team bench, and dramatically overturns a chair; is it comedic or sad? *see Hidden Curriculum, Quaint Ideas/Quaint Technology, Volunteer Labor.*

BEER This beverage can make a person feel animated, at least for a time. Teachers should avoid pouring it in coffee, stashing it in the classroom file cabinet, or when assigned to a high school, selling it to students; *see Filing Cabinet, I Don't Know (Poor Responses-b), GPA, Marking (a), Teachers' High, Watering Hole, Yearbook.*

BEGINNER BAND / ORCHESTRA The best adult musicians had to start somewhere. It was unlikely that their instruments sounded crisp and clean the first time they blew on a horn, pulled a bow across a violin, or pounded on the drums. The sound of one beginner butchering a musical instrument is difficult to tolerate. It is almost unfathomable that the teacher must listen to twenty-five or thirty rookies at the same time. The poor soul does not even have the luxury of wearing ear plugs, these having a detrimental impact on the ability to teach the class. It is important to remember the sacrifices these teachers made the next time one is enjoying professionally played music, either at a concert or recorded on a tech device.

BENCHMARKING Teachers are not business people. If they were, the benchmarking of student ability would replicate corporate predictions of forward earnings, which are almost always on the meager side. The low earnings guidance enables the CFO (Chief Financial Officer), to shine several months hence, boasting that the corporation's quarterly earnings exceeded expectations. If teachers caught on to such shenanigans and were able to bury a few bothersome ethical issues, low beginning benchmarks would enable them to boast at year-end. Their students could easily "exceed expectations" by having increased their reading or numeracy proficiency at a rate far greater than that normally expected in a single school year; *see Accountability, Diving Into the Data, Number Fudgers, Quantification.*

BIAS OVER BALANCE Forsaking any semblance of a balanced approach to a topic, a tiny minority of high school teachers occasionally use the classroom as a pulpit, advocating a plethora of social and political causes. Having heard a similar sonorous speech many times in the past, the students may revert to more important concerns such as flirting, texting, or sleeping. On the few occasions when such audience ambivalence is noticed, the proselytizing teacher is left to complain about apathetic youth, vowing to ramp up the harangue in the next "lesson"; *see Guest Speaker Negativity, Politicos, Texting.*

BLACKBOARDS In an interesting twist on language, teachers kept referring to these classroom spaces as blackboards when for decades they had been green. These have largely been replaced by whiteboards, which are, thankfully white; *see Chalk, Whiteboards.*

BLAME INDUSTRY Just as lawyers are cornerstone participants in the conflict business, teachers are key personnel in the blame industry. There is no end of societal ills that can be laid at teachers' doorstep. A decline in reading or spelling scores is the school's fault and has nothing to do with television or the gibberish spelling used in texting. The increase in the number of overweight children is the school's failure as well; a result of poor PE instruction and not the prevalence of junk food. So too, schools can be blamed for increased drug usage and pregnancy rates amongst teens, any decline in voter participation, and general absence of manners amongst the young. Being on the front line of student contact, teachers are natural targets and will frequently hear the media jackals cry, "It's the school's fault"; *see Education (Public), Fault Police, Journalists, Insurance Investigations, Politicians, Testing (Standardized).*

BLENDED FAMILIES Some veteran colleagues may remember a time when students usually lived with two parents who cohabited for more than six months. This is no longer the case. Many have extended families. Unlike traditional cultures, the family does not live under one roof and the members keep changing with frequency resembling participants on a TV game show. This makes any attempt at understanding the student's family dynamics virtually impossible. Communication with the parents can be an additional challenge. Which parent should the teacher choose to divulge information? Will that parent communicate with the other? Teachers are advised to duplicate and triplicate the notices sent home; *see Conflict (Parental), Counselors, Graduation, Hard Copy, I Don't Know (Good Responses-b).*

BOSS A teacher has more bosses than candles in a Catholic church. There are the taxpayers who foot the bill, as well as their representatives at the government and school board levels. Parents, who are "consuming the service," can be especially bossy and demanding. A teacher has immediate supervisors (the secretary and the janitor), mid-level managers (the vice-principal and principal), and school board big-shots, (curriculum directors, assistant or associate superintendents and the superintendent of schools). Bossing teachers around must be particularly enjoyable work since a considerable number of people are in on the action; *see Curriculum Coordinators, Government Interference, Instant Response, Janitor, Occupational Hazards (f/g), Office Workers, Parent Council (b), Principal (b), School Board Members, Self-Esteem (Teacher), Vice-Principal.*

BRAINSTORMING A popular activity at teacher meetings when all the participants talk at once and behave in a manner none would approve of if duplicated by their students; *see Consensus, Kings and Queens, Principal (e), Quagmire, Yappers (1/2).*

BUBBLE WRAP KIDS It's an adventure to be a kid; literally, since no child wants to live in a cocoon. That type of existence is for old people, like grandparents; or teachers. Childhood is a time for climbing trees, and finding snakes in a vacant lot or field, and running in the rain, and stomping on mud puddles. All these activities are tough to do when you're wrapped in plastic; *see Fault Police, Helicopter Parents.*

BUDGET This ultimate decision-maker often acts in a mysterious, authoritarian manner. Phrases such as "The budget won't allow it", or "We have to check with the budget", are frequently heard. At times soft persuasion can influence this omnipotent entity, exemplified by the phrases, "We've worked on the budget and it can handle this", or "We'll see if we can massage the budget a bit", the latter comment opening up a number of questions about physical contact best left dormant. On the rare occasion when the deity provides additional money for a classroom or program, it is wise not to ask questions; *see Advertising, Back-to-School Sales, Zero (b).*

BUDGING IN LINE Anxious to be at the front of the queue, those primary age children skipping ahead of others will receive the wrath of the always-present squealers. These tattle-tale students will demand that the teacher punish the offender with torture only slightly less arduous than the rack. The teacher will want to follow their demands, but by applying the suggested discipline to the whiners rather than those who had budged; *see Kayaks and Canoes, Rule Breakers (2), Tattlers and Squealers.*

BULLYING BEHAVIOR What qualifies as examples of this ugly behavior has altered considerably. In the past, bullying was relatively easy to discern, though not always acted on as swiftly or effectively as it could have been. However, what used to be thought of as taunting and playground spats may now be regarded by many parents as outrageous examples of malicious bullying. Their "bullied" child has been offended and could carry permanent emotional scars. Blood must be spilled against the alleged perpetrator. In the zeal for vengeance, the demands of the victim's parents mimic the worst of bullying behavior; *see Fault Police, Helicopter Parents, Playground Spats.*

C

CAMEL With all due respect to the animal, the oft-described origin of the somewhat ugly, snarling, ill-tempered beast was that it was a horse designed by a committee. One can only imagine what a creature devised by a specialized education committee would look like; *see Laws of Bureaucracy (4).*

CAMPING The national and state park services advertise camping as a family adventure, with a likely assumption that a family has one to five children. An elementary class camping trip includes twenty-five children, many of whom are on their first outdoor experience. This mob is supervised by one teacher accompanied by parent volunteers who may or may not be helpful; now *that* is an adventure; *see Field Trips (b), Kayaks and Canoes.*

CARPETING Normally ultra-sensitive to student health and safety, primary teachers frequently lose common sense regarding floor covering for reading centers, seemingly oblivious to the dirt and dross in carpets. The fibers suck in germs from student coughs and sneezes, the saliva from licking tongues, and the juice from child lunches; not to mention the usual grime lurking in the threads and weaves. The reading-center rug is seldom cleaned and then only in the summer when the teacher is not there to see the thick black goo that is pulled from the liquid vacuum cleaner; *see Juice, Oranges, Occupational Hazards (a), Sneeze, UFO (2).*

CHALK This is an ancient writing implement used on blackboards. It caused teachers to have dry hands, dust on the edges of pant pockets, and fits of coughing and wheezing. Relegated to the chalk-dust bin of history, a discarded piece, with an accompanying brush, may be found tucked in a corner of a seldom-used storage room; *see Blackboards, Non-Verbal Communication, Occupational Hazards (a), Pencils, Quaint Ideas/Quaint Technology (2), Whiteboards.*

CLASSROOM MANAGEMENT An important teacher skill previously accomplished through the use of medieval strategies such as straps, canes, and belts. These were applied to students who had the ability to pay attention longer than the time between commercials on TV. Now, activities that can accomplish some semblance of quiet behavior in students is to turn on a television or DVD and watch as students drift into a trance-like stupor; *see Jason, Halo, Nano-Second, Noise, Non-Verbal*

Communication, Notes in Class, Pareto Principle, Television Screen, UFO (1).

CLUBS These school activities should not be confused with clubbing as in, "Pounding a person on the head with a stick" or, "Drinking and dancing the night away in an alcoholic haze." For decades school clubs were relatively innocuous. All that was required was a teacher willing to volunteer time to sponsor and organize a group of interested students. Twenty years ago, very few teachers would have predicted the formation of LGBTQ clubs (Lesbian, Gay, Bi-sexual, Trans and Queer), that have sprouted in high schools to promote much-needed tolerance. Looking to the future, occasional censorship may be required to thwart the formation of groups such as the Young Nazis or the Satanic Youth League; *see Volunteer Labor.*

COFFEE FUND Some colleagues avoid these dues by bringing their own java in a thermos, claiming that the coffee in the staffroom is undrinkable. As true as that may be, the real reason is that they do not wish to contribute to the fund. Many colleagues do not pay until year end; some not at all. The unending debates over the coffee fund will take up an extraordinary amount of staff meeting time yet reach no resolution. This type of inconclusive yakking mirrors much of the verbiage that flows from congressional debates; *see Coffee Machine, Instant Response, Investment Club, Java, Lunch at a Restaurant, Mug, Quagmire.*

COFFEE MACHINE A stimulant dispensing unit, this valuable device holds a place of prominence and receives appropriate reverence in the staffroom; *see Coffee Fund, Java, Mug, Recess, Valium, Veteran Teachers (d).*

COMPUTER-ASSISTED INSTRUCTION The turn-of-the-millennium excitement about the technological possibilities of computers was similar to 1960's educational furor about television revolutionizing teaching. Given the abysmal quality of the majority of television programming, that revolution, if it existed at all, was uninspiring at best; *see Techno-Geeks, Television, Television Screen.*

CONFLICT (PARENTAL) Occasionally a teacher will be emotionally yanked between two conflicting parents seeking support for their point of view regarding a child's development. Staying in the neutral middle ground is essential. Some strategies teachers can employ are; being oblivious, whether real or faked, or insisting everyone involved meet at the same time thus providing referee status. Another handy alternative is referring the matter to the principal, who, after all, gets the "big bucks" to deal with such issues; *see Blended Families, Counselors, Graduation, I Don't Know (Good Responses-b), Potential, Principal.*

CONSENSUS A term used to describe the majority of decisions made at meetings when all the loud-mouthed, opinionated colleagues agree. After hearing these staff members, who usually comprise no more than ten percent of those present, the principal will usually conclude, "Right then, it seems that we have consensus. Let's move on to the next item on the agenda." The process will then repeat itself and the principal will regard his or her action as evidence of effective "consensus-building"; *see Cooperative Learning, Division (b), Principal (e), Queen Bee, Recycling, Rural Schools (One Room).*

CONSERVATIVE-THINKING LIBERALS Public school teachers naturally lean toward political parties that favor higher levels of government spending. Despite the majority of teachers leaning liberal-left from a broad political perspective, the contrast with the specifics of teacher behavior on the job provides an interesting juxtaposition. Teachers have a steady if unspectacular income, as opposed to the fluctuations inherent in sales or operating a small business. They manage and control the workday of other people (students). They wear relatively dull, conformist attire and drive practical vehicles. They seek hierarchical support from their supervisor (principal), for whatever sanctions they have levied against those they control (students). These workplace nuances are more consistent with individuals who are conventional or even conservative in thinking; *see Dress, Fads (Fashion), Kings and Queens, One-Trick Pony, Uniformity of Thought, Versace, Gucci, and Armani (b).*

COOPERATIVE LEARNING With students of different abilities and interests working together in small groups, this strategy can be excellent glue to bind elementary age children. Alas, as students mature, they work hard to establish a defined identity. If the group of adolescents is too disparate, there is a chance that the well-planned activities may not be effective. High school "jocks" may be loath to work in a group made up of largely of "smoke pit dopers." Automotive "grease monkeys" may balk at being placed in a group with a high number of theater "nerds." Eager to be in charge of their own fate and guarantee the quality of the eventual project, academic students may want to work in splendid isolation. High school teachers understand the challenge. The staff diversity in a large high school can make cooperative activities amongst the teachers a challenge as well; *see Consensus, Kings and Queens.*

COUNSELORS No classes, no marking, and no report cards. This sounds like a great "teaching" job until one realizes that dealing with seriously behaviorally-challenged students and/or parents all day is not fun, especially when everyone expects a magic wand to be waved that will make the issues disappear in a puff of smoke. These professionals tend to listen well. Unlike administrators, they are adept enough at reflective listening to avoid being obvious and driving the speaker bonkers. Out of necessity, counselors are often very adept at psychobabble and spouting on about syndromes and disorders which defy answers and/or cures; *see Blended Families, Conflict (Parental), Edubabble, Librarian, Psychobabble, Reflective Listening, Syndrome.*

CRITICAL THINKING SKILLS Be careful what one wishes for! It may be fashionable edubabble for a teacher to focus on critical thinking skills but one might be in for a rude shock when the students use those new-found skills to critique the instructional performance to which they have been subjected. Like Dr. Frankenstein, who created a life-force he could not control, high levels of student critical thinking capability can have unintended negative repercussions. It is difficult to turn off the critical thinking tap once the juice has started to flow; *see Frankenstein, Questions (Student).*

CURRICULUM This is the material to be taught as determined by non-teachers chatting amiably in a distant government office. In the real world of the classroom there is little time for idle chit-chat as "covering" the curriculum will require twice the time allotted; *see Curriculum Coordinators, Expert, Politicians, Relevance, Safety Education.*

CURRICULUM COORDINATORS Working at the school board office, these people do not teach. They "coordinate" the work of those who do. They are extremely adept at edubabble, a main requirement for the job. Because of the supposed higher level of job complexity, these professionals usually receive more pay than classroom teachers. They are also able to hobnob with others who don't work in a school but regard themselves to be at the cutting edge of education. Occasionally they are selected for state-wide committees tasked with launching a massive curricular change of dubious value; *see Boss, Edubabble, Expert, Job Interview (d), Laws of Bureaucracy (3), Yappers (2).*

CUSTODIAN *see Janitor, Names and Titles.*

D

DANCE

1. This student social extravaganza is accompanied by deafening sounds, very few of which resemble music. Those teacher chaperones who are on the north side of forty are advised to wear earplugs; *see Full Moon Theorist, Jive Dancing, Volunteer Labor.*
2. Uncoordinated yet entertaining moves are often performed by teachers on the last day of the school year. Jigs are the most common type, followed by line dances. Tangos should be avoided and lap dancing is definitely taboo unless one has tenure; *see Educational Correctness.*

DATA-DRIVEN DECISION MAKING Occasionally initials are an excellent indication of the usefulness and/or shelf life of an educational trend. This style of decision making; DDDM, seems to be dangerously close to an amalgam of DDT and ICBM; *see Abbreviations,*

Accountability, Benchmarking, Diving Into the Data, Expert, Number Crunchers, Number Fudgers, Politicians.

DE BONO This is not the Bono of peace-activist, rock-star notoriety, but rather a British psychologist, famous for emphasizing people's ability to shift laterally from one idea to another. De Bono's lateral thinking work is often linked to creativity, which is a trait he likely shares with the Bono of U2 fame.

DENSE This word describes people in a less-than-flattering manner, with the following examples unfortunately found in a few schools:

a) a principal who fails to understand the positive and practical idea a teacher has proposed, favoring a convoluted busy-work model instead; *see Principal (e);*

b) a student who frequently demonstrates ridiculous behavior such as putting a tongue on an icy flag pole, leaping over the high-jump bar without a landing mat, or field-testing the amount of glue necessary to weld fingers together; *see Frozen Tongues;*

c) a teacher who does not preview a movie that was rented from the adult section of the video store; *see DVDs, Lingerie.*

DESIGN

1. An exclusively male activity, school design "boasts" virtually no storage or closet space, no full-length

mirrors in staff restrooms, almost no counter or cupboard space in the staffroom, and walls covered in paint colors acquired from the cheapest case lot sale at the big-box discount warehouse. Female teachers might consider a career move to architecture and design; *see Linoleum.*

2. Though the box-like school structures of 1950's and 1960's lacked any redeeming architectural features, the rooms were wonderfully large to accommodate the class sizes of the era and were flooded with natural light from expansive windows; *see Windows (b).*
3. Contemporary school design features considerable architectural appeal with impressive foyers and rotundas "stolen" from the square footage previously allotted to individual classrooms. The end result is laughably small teaching spaces, but at least the school has "street appeal"; *see Windows (c).*

DESK As in the home, furniture can be a status symbol. The teacher desk is usually larger than those occupied by students and may even have a drawer or two. By mid-September the top will be piled with paper and the ugly brown desktop will not be visible until the last school day of the year. The mounds of paper are more aesthetically pleasing than the scratched and gouged wood veneer. If the desk is substandard and there is a measure of rapport with the janitor, a teacher may be able to successfully plead for a newer model; *see Hard Copy, Janitor, Keys.*

DESKS (STUDENT) One of the iron laws of teaching is that no matter how many student desks are in your room on the first day of school, the number will be two less than the number of students assigned to your class. A second law of teaching is at least two of the student desks in your room will be too large, or too small, for any of the students.

DEWEY DECIMAL SYSTEM Not aware of the philosophical work of John Dewey (below), many teachers might regard him as the father of the library cataloguing system. That honor, however, falls to Melvil Dewey in 1876; *see Library.*

DEWEY, JOHN A teacher will likely recognize the following contemporary ideas: experiential learning, integrated curriculum, a strong emphasis on problem solving and critical thinking skills, personalized learning, group work, the development of social skills, and social responsibility. These were the cornerstones of the progressive education movement of which John Dewey was a recognized leader. Contemporary as the above pedagogical emphasis appears, Dewey's most influential works were written between 1890 and 1920; *see Quotes on Education/Ancient Greek Philosophers.*

DIPHTHONG People may believe that primary teachers are too busy to be spending time tossing around edubabble. However, oft-used phrases such as "play-based learning" and "phonemic awareness" demonstrate that these teachers are capable at firing off some impressive-sounding jargon of their own. They even know the meaning of words like diphthong, which puts them ahead of most middle school teachers and virtually all colleagues at the high school level. That the term is borrowed from linguistics is of no concern. Educators spouting psychobabble frequently steal from the lexicon of other disciplines; *see Pareto Principle, Psychobabble, Quality Circles, Q-Sort.*

DIVING INTO THE DATA This slogan has been popularized by number crunchers having dived head first into the shallow end of the swimming pool once too often. It is helpful to recall the oft-paraphrased line from Nobel prize-winning British economist Ronald Coase, "If you torture the data long enough, it will confess"; *see Accountability, Benchmarking, Data-Driven Decision Making, Number Crunchers, Office Workers, Principal (d).*

DIVISION A supposedly easily understood term that nonetheless can pose the following comprehension difficulties:

a) an arithmetic concept that some students will never understand, no matter how many times it is taught to them;

b) a method of organizing an elementary school into classes, a process that some teachers will never understand, no matter how many times it is outlined to them; *see Consensus, Queen Bee, Random Selection;*

c) the organization of the governance system in education into jurisdictional units (also called districts), which some members of the public will never understand, no matter how many times it is explained to them; *see Jurisdiction.*

DONUTS In an era of culinary correctness these calorie-laden treats have been eliminated from staff-meeting snacks in favor of cucumber sandwiches, gluten-free flax muffins, and melon slices. Veteran colleagues lament the loss of the sugar highs of yesteryear which enabled them to stay awake for at least a portion of the meeting. Scarfing down a donut seemed far less embarrassing than sonorous snoring; *see Food Police (a), Nourishment.*

DRAMATIC PERFORMANCE A form of artistic expression, the best moments occur away from the theatrical stage and can be viewed in the day-to-day work life of a school. Some prime examples include:

a) the principal explaining to staff and parents why the latest budget cuts will actually be good for the school; *see Budget, Leadership Bull;*

b) the early adolescent students who flirt, become a couple, and break up before noon on the same day; *see Eighth-Grade Boys, Hallway Conversations,*

Hormones With Feet, Middle School, No Man's Land, Notes in Class, Seventh-Grade Girls;

c) the politician announcing the latest major initiative for public education; *see Boss, Expert, Government Interference, Innovation, Politician;*

d) the veteran teacher delivering a retirement speech, describing the sadness about leaving the profession and entering a life of leisure; *see Pension Knowledge, Veteran Teachers (e).*

DRESS Except for the wise sage, jackets and ties for men and dresses and skirts for women have disappeared from school attire. Teachers may consider visiting the local discount store in August to ascertain the teacher fashion trends for the coming year; *see Back-to-School Sales, Flip Flops (1), Conservative-Thinking Liberals, Fads (Fashion), Goth Look, Investment Club, Jeans, Jocks and Jockettes, Versace, Gucci, and Armani, Wise Sage.*

DUTY Whether it be playground, bus, hallway, or exam supervision, this task is never fun. Clever veteran colleagues schedule their after-school duty on staff meeting days, thus avoiding at least a portion of another unpleasant responsibility. Other veteran tricks include snagging duty on Friday when student absenteeism is higher; *see Rain Days, Kung Fu, Playground Spats, Recess, Veteran Teachers, X-Box.*

DVDS Given enough experience, any teacher can learn to justify showing a movie by linking it to at least a few government-prescribed learning outcomes. Restricted movies should be avoided, particularly in elementary school. Save these for the staff social; *see Beer, Dense (c), Lingerie.*

DYSCALCULIA On occasion edubabble can really be of benefit. It can enable educators to sound more knowledgeable and current than they really are. It can bafflegab parents and keep them at bay. It can add a few big words to a project proposal. And as a bonus, it can enable a weakness to sound strikingly clinical. It is not uncommon for teachers to display low levels of understanding regarding budget issues. More than a few had to repeat the education statistics course three times. Some struggle to calculate marks. Given all this, it is clear that more than a few teachers suffer with dyscalculia, a learning disability which is an inability to comprehend arithmetic. Admitting to colleagues that one has a "tinge of dyscalculia," sounds far more impressive than, "I suck at numbers"; *see Math for the Masses, Median, Standard Deviation, Zero (c).*

E

EDUBABBLE This form of educator communication involves the use of ridiculously fluffy words and silly sloganeering intended to obfuscate issues and confuse non-educators. Colleague reaction to edubabble is antithetical. Some teachers roll exasperated eyes and snort derisively while others nod deferentially to those proficient in its use; *see Curriculum Coordinators, Expert, Inquiry-Based Learning, Leading Edge, Quest for Excellence, Robust, Visionary, Yappers (2).*

EDUCATIONAL CORRECTNESS (EC) The EC borders are as real as the former Berlin Wall; and definitely more successful in accomplishing the desired outcome. Like its cousins, political and culinary correctness (PC and CC), EC provides the acceptable limits to debate, discussion, and discourse. Unlike tangible blockades, these walls are unlikely to come crashing down and appear to become stronger and higher as the years progress. This drives most common sense, almost all humor, and the best conversations from the staffroom to the watering hole on Friday afternoons; *see Jokes, Kipling, Novels, Phonics, Renegades, Uniformity of Thought, Valentine's Day, Watering Hole, Workplace Poisoning.*

EDUCATION (PRIVATE) Most people would question any business that costs twice as much to operate yet only produces a marginally better product. Somehow private schools have managed to avoid such financial scrutiny. With often more than twice the revenue than their public-school counterparts (inputs), on average their students only marginally surpass the level of exam achievement of public schools (outputs). From a purely investment-for-return perspective, private schools are a bust; *see Accountability, Education (Public), Voucher System.*

EDUCATION PROFESSORS It is a wonder that several politicians, and even a few teachers, listen to what these people have to say. With a few exceptions these "experts" in teaching have rarely, if ever, taught in a public-school classroom. They work in an environment where research is more valued than teaching competence. Their attempts to make education a respected research discipline have been unsuccessful. They occupy one of the lowest rungs on the university status ladder, battling it out with the Sociology professors to avoid falling to the bottom position; *see Assessment for Learning/Assessment of Learning, Edubabble, Expert, Illich, Inquiry-Based Learning, Nadir, University (2), Visionary, Workshops and Seminars.*

EDUCATION (PUBLIC) Perhaps the greatest social triumph of the previous century, public education is not quick, easy, problem-free, or inexpensive to operate; challenges shared though less scrutinized, by another publicly-funded enterprise; the military. Given that the citizenry desires rapid results, demands simple explanations and dislikes paying taxes, it is clear why the education system receives abnormal levels of angst over funding; *see Blame Industry, Education (Private), Societal Expectations, Voucher System, Zeitgeist.*

EIGHTH-GRADE BOYS At one time these students might have been interested in schoolwork; but not now. Suddenly, to these boys, previously ignored body parts, both their own and those of others, appear to have changed. Girls look different; *really* different. Even Miss Newsom, the young Science teacher seems to have changed, and that is too weird to even talk about. Hair grows where there was none before. The brain keeps telling the tongue to question almost everything an adult says. Previously smoothly toned arms and legs display muscle bulges and there is a sudden urge to use them to push people around.

Good luck to the teacher trying to teach this tortured human being; *see Dramatic Performance (b), Hormones With Feet, Middle School, No Man's Land, Notes in Class, Pension Knowledge, Seventh-Grade Girls.*

EINSTEIN, ALBERT The notion that Albert Einstein failed Mathematics is frequently used to demonstrate how ineffective the school system is and how clueless the teachers are who work in it. Alas, Einstein did not fail Mathematics. Not surprisingly he was a proficient Math and Physics student, a fact his teachers noted. He did however, chafe at the rigidity of the school system of the day, particularly when being instructed in other subjects. Though he failed the entrance exam to the Zurich Polytechnic on his first attempt, he wrote the exam at an earlier age than most students. While scoring well in Mathematics and Physics, Einstein failed the Botany, Zoology and Language sections. Notably, the examination was written in French, a language Einstein did not know well. This perhaps casts a questionable light on post-secondary entrance requirements rather than the alleged inability of teachers to detect a genius; *see Gifted.*

ELECTRONIC COMMUNICATION

1. It is extremely difficult for a teacher to be an effective communicator when so awash in emails that he or she does not have the time to read them, let alone respond; *see I Generation, Instant Response, Knee-Deep Syndrome, Memo.*
2. It is extremely difficult to be an effective communicator when teachers are not able to use inflection or non-verbal language. Electronic information transfer may be impressively speedy but cannot match effective human communication in substance and style; *see Grapevine, Learning Suite, Names and Titles, Non-Verbal Communication.*

ELEMENTARY SCHOOL CONCERTS It is impossible to be impartial when viewing these performances. Virtually everyone in the audience is either a family member of a child on stage, or a teacher at the school. Kindergarten and early primary performances are notably entertaining. Some children wave enthusiastically to mothers in the audience while others stand statue-skill in the glare of the lights. A few mine nostrils and others show a need to use bathroom facilities. This all occurs as the teacher bravely attempts to assist the children in the singing and choreography that had been so assiduously rehearsed in class.

The performance of older elementary students, who no longer can compete on the cute scale with primary children and are not able to perform with a skill level to match even early adolescents, is impartially speaking, worth the price of admission; which is free.

EMERGENCY PREPAREDNESS In a bygone era, the most notable emergency most schools faced was a conflagration, making fire drills commonplace. With societal violence escalating at a frightening pace, lockdown procedures and drills are now a necessary part of school life. Probably more than anything else, this is a sad comment on the direction which American society has taken; *see Bottleneck, Fire Drills, Gum, Health and Safety, Jamming and Cramming, Nurturing Environment.*

EMPOWERMENT This management idea involves four times the work for a teacher for the same amount of pay.

By involving teachers in everything, they feel important and respected, or so the reasoning goes. Instead, teachers are burdened with more committees, more meetings, and more discussions that lack conclusion about topics that lack substance. All the while the teacher is expected to continue with regular classroom duties while supposedly feeling much better about doing so. This empowerment movement is intended to build morale while the hierarchy remains intact; *see Innovation, Quality Circles, Q-Sort.*

ENCYCLOPEDIA ONLINE An invaluable repository of accurate, factual information, this source provides hordes of students with complete written reports in a writing style eerily similar to Wikipedia. There is hope however. Given enough practice, students will eventually plagiarize as well as their teachers did in a previous era; *see University.*

ENVIRONMENTAL CORRECTNESS Closely related to its political, educational, and culinary cousins, many of the most vociferous supporters drive SUV's or camper vans to school each day; *see Non-Carbon Paper, Recycling, Vinyl Lunch Bags.*

ETHNOCENTRISM It is gratifying to witness the slow demise of the seriously ethnocentric views of history that used to dominate American curriculum. World War II did not start with the bombing of Pearl Harbor, having being waged for more than two years before that event. Bygone-era textbooks used the term "Dark Ages" to describe the period prior to the Renaissance (the rebirth is an ethnocentric term itself), ignoring the fact that many civilizations prospered at the time and were at the forefront of humankind's development, examples being Chinese and Moorish triumphs. The notion that Columbus "discovered" America now seems quaint since it is logical to assume that the native inhabitants of what is now the Caribbean islands had already "discovered" where they lived.

EXAMINATION In schools these episodic events are usually less embarrassing, though more public, than those in medical labs or hospitals. Education or medical results may bring similar student reactions ranging from giddy happiness to depression. Unlike a medical exam, cheating is much easier in a school exam and the participant is usually clothed.

EXAM WEEK While the English, History, Science, Mathematics, and Language teachers mark exams, and the Woodwork, Mechanics, and Foods teachers clean their labs and shops, the Physical Education teachers have time to talk about sports and swap tales about the athletic glory days of their youth.

EXCUSES It is as if there is a website for student excuses. After a few years, a teacher would have heard all the standard woes of misfortune that caused work to be incomplete or the machinations of others that caused tardiness or misbehavior. It is understandable to wish for a few truly creative flights of fancy such as, "I'm not late, I'm early for tomorrow," or, "I didn't hear the bell. I have wax-accretion syndrome," or, "I didn't do the essay. I'm into environmental issues and don't believe in wasting paper." There are other memorable classics to provide a little spice to a dull day, such as, "I didn't hit him. He stepped into my fist on the playground," or, "It's wasn't my booze. Some big guys held me on the ground and poured it down my throat"; *see Untruthful Statements, Yarn.*

EXEMPLAR Despite the name, exemplars are not examples of superb work. However, exemplars could be exceedingly excellent as an extra tool to examine examples of student progress. The alliteration in that edubabble does not get much better.

EXPERT A title reserved for those who don't work in schools but have much to say about education; *see Curriculum Coordinators, Education Professors, Edubabble, Innovation, Job Interview (d), Laws of Bureaucracy (c), Nadir, Opinion, Politicians, Politicos.*

F

FADS (EDUCATIONAL) An educational fad will come, go and return with a new, more impressive name. After a time, the craze will fall into disrepute. It will assuredly re-emerge, Phoenix-like, with an even more majestic moniker; *see Flip Flops (2), Innovation, Open Area Classrooms/Open Concept School, Principal (f), Reflective Listening.*

FADS (FASHION) Working in a high school allows a teacher to be aware of the latest teen fashion trends, from bell bottom pants in the sixties to disco-inspired polyester in the seventies. By the eighties there was "big hair" and ripped clothing for girls and thin ties for boys. The nineties saw a fair share of the grunge-rock look. Hoodies and rap-influenced clothing came with the new century. While young teachers may wish to appear cool and participate in the fashion derby, this is not recommended. Thirty-year-old teachers may try too hard and look silly or, even worse, appear "creepy" (male), or "sleazy" (female). Young teachers should also not try to emulate the jackets and ties or shapeless dresses of the wise sage, since that too will appear strange. Stick to classic teacher fashion; conservative, relatively cheap, and slightly out-of-style. Teacher attire works best when it is not noticed; *see Conservative-Thinking Liberals, Dress, Goth Look, Jeans, Jocks and Jockettes, Versace, Gucci, and Armani, Wise Sage.*

FAULT POLICE Any small bump, bruise, cut, scrape, or blister damaging the child's bubble-wrapped body is akin to tortuous physical agony that may require surgery. Any minor ego-deflation, sad feelings, or hurtful words is likened to traumatic psychological pain that may require counseling intervention. Fault must lie somewhere, blame be apportioned and the demon exorcised. The "time-vampire" parents who engage in such shenanigans should be a feature on *Saturday Night Live* rather than taking up the teacher's time in an after-school meeting; *see Blame Industry, Bubble Wrap Kids, Bullying Behavior, Helicopter Parents, Idioms, Insurance Investigations, Journalists, Self-Esteem (Teacher).*

FIDGET These quick jerky movements are made by bored students providing non-verbal signals that they have no interest in the lesson a teacher has spent an hour preparing. Teachers of adolescents will soon observe various techno-gadgets being pulled from pockets, followed by eyes focused downward before thumb tapping begins in earnest. Colleagues will notice the same behavior from millennial-aged teachers during staff meetings as the oblivious principal babbles on; *see Assembly, Classroom Management, Jason, Occupational Hazards (e), Principal (d), Techno-Gadgets.*

FIELD TRIPS To ensure sanity during these high-risk adventures, teachers should adhere to these important rules:

a) know the route to the anticipated destination. Wandering aimlessly with a bus load of children is only exciting for the first thirty seconds;

b) return with all the students. No matter how enticing it may be to leave a few behind, their parents usually want them home; *see Camping, Kayaks and Canoes;*

c) avoid visual contact with a fast food outlet less than sixty minutes prior to lunch; *see Food Police, Lunch Sales, Pizza.*

FILING CABINET This metallic container is coated in the dullest color possible and sits stoically in a corner of the classroom. Over time, it becomes a repository of valuable, and not so valuable, material. The worth of the cabinet increases if the lock works, and skyrockets if the janitor is willing to part with the only key that opens it; *see Janitor, Keys.*

FIRE DRILL There is little point in everyone charging out of the school in a frenzied rush, so the practice of orderly exit is important for the safety of all concerned.

These drills should include staff exit procedures on Friday afternoons; *see Bottleneck, Emergency Preparedness, Health and Safety, Invigilating, Jamming and Cramming, Watering Hole.*

FIRST-YEAR TEACHER Similar to articling in law or residency in medicine, the energetic wide-eyed idealist in September can morph into a bleary-eyed pragmatist by February. The beginner is often loaded with the school's most difficult assignment to test the rookie's mettle. Full teacher status is conferred upon survival at year end; *see Keener, Tests (New Teacher).*

FITBIT On any given day a primary teacher will be up, down, over, and under; as well as walking, standing, arranging, pinning, tying, drawing, writing, coloring, monitoring, speaking, pointing, and laughing. That, and much more, will be completed before recess. Monitoring activity levels to gauge the rate of calorie-burn is not necessary. The average primary teacher does not have the time.

FLIP FLOPS

1. This footwear is not recommended clothing for the classroom, particularly in winter in most regions of North America; *see Dress.*
2. This type of maneuvering is typical of politicians, administrators, union leaders, and school board members when the idea they had championed

has failed miserably; *see Innovation, Leading Edge, Principal (f), Zig-Zag (2).*

FLUORESCENT LIGHTING The preferred lighting in schools makes a distinctive, loud hum on the first two days of school that goes unnoticed for the remainder of the year. When tired it tends to blink on and off, giving a surreal effect resembling a cheap version of strobe lighting; *see Design.*

FRILLS One person's frill can be another person's core. Few people disagree that literacy and numeracy are the pillars of learning, with the Sciences trailing not far behind. After that, a debate ensues. Reasonable arguments can be made that Art, Foods and Nutrition, Geography, History, Languages, Music, Performance, Physical Education, and Technology should be priorities and not be considered the frills that they often are. Alas, only in education can every subject be regarded as being a priority, thus defeating the meaning of the word; *see Art, Budget, Relevance, Robotics.*

FOOD POLICE

1. Not lagging far behind on the political and educational correctness scale is the culinary variety. There are usually at least a few members on staff ready to correct any colleague for bringing a lunch in a paper bag and pounce on a principal who brings donuts to a staff meeting. They issue a gentle reprimand to colleagues who defrost

store-bought pizza in the staffroom microwave or pour three spoons of white sugar into coffee mugs. Miscreant teachers should ensure that any consumption of potato chips and cheezies is done in the privacy of the classroom at break times; *see Donuts, Educational Correctness, Microwave, Vinyl Lunch Bags.*

2. If the food police had authority over the parent council which organizes the hot dog and pizza sales, they would convert student lunches to quinoa salad and tofu burgers; *see Field Trip (c), Hot Dogs, Lunch Sales, Nourishment, Parent Council, Pizza, Recess.*

FOOTBALL TEAM Unlike exemplary learning programs and quality teaching, the football team receives a great deal of local media coverage which enhances positive public relations and burnishes the school image. Young men can let off a little steam so they are not butting heads in the hallway or brawling in the change room. Thanks to football, the school can encourage aggression and mayhem while charging a fee for people wishing to watch; *see Gender-Based Sports, Golf Team, Oxymorons, Recruiting, Testosterone Poisoning.*

FRANKENSTEIN The movies have given Mary Shelley's "monster" a bad rap. Admittedly the fellow might have lacked adequate social graces, but the main issue of the tale was Dr. Frankenstein's inability to control his creation. It might be a good idea for high school teachers to be equally wary of controlling the "creatures" that arise from their instructional efforts. A student who is adept in Electricity class may learn to disarm the front doors of the local liquor mart. The knowledge acquired in Computer class may enable him or her to hack into the school's computer system and alter student marks. The extra lung capacity developed in PE class will be helpful in making a quick getaway from a robbery. The numeracy knowledge will be handy in ensuring a profit from the booty. In case of capture, the debating skills honed in English class will come in handy in extricating him or herself from time in the local jail.

There is a fine line between a difficult-to-control, youthful "monster" and a "renaissance teen" bound for glory in the world of business; *see Critical Thinking Skills, Number Fudgers, Rule Breakers (1).*

FROZEN TONGUES Stuck to popsicles, flag poles, ice cubes, freezers, metal railings, and car bumpers; is there any place some students, young or old, will not place their tongues? *see Dense (b).*

FRUIT FLIES Some unwelcome creatures appreciate the ample food source found in old, though not discarded, lunches. Unwelcome as they are, fruit flies can swarm the school unless there are regular locker, classroom, and/or cloakroom clean-outs. These annoying bugs can lay up to five hundred eggs in their short life span of just over a week, making an amorous rabbit seem celibate in comparison. Even the janitor may be defeated by the bug infestation. Contracting external pest removal specialists may be necessary; *see Apples, Health and Safety, Janitor, Oranges, Recycling, UFO (2).*

FULL MOON THEORIST It takes one boozy, fight-filled high school dance held on full moon nights to turn any teacher sponsor of the student council into a believer in the negative power of this lunar phase. Even the most rational individual will succumb to the apparent causality and always ensure that the dance is scheduled as far away from a full moon as possible; *see Dance (1), Volunteer Labor.*

FUNCTIONAL LITERACY It is not feasible, and perhaps not even desirable, to have all graduating students reading novels written by the literary greats. The economy depends upon a large population of literate adults, but not *too* literate. Someone has to buy the tabloids at grocery store checkout counters and gorge on celebrity gossip. Someone has to consume the sports pages of newspapers. Someone has to buy *People Magazine* and pay the ridiculous cover price given that eighty percent of the page space is filled with advertising; *see Grisham, Harlequin Romance (2), Reading (Technical Manuals).*

G

GENDER-BASED SPORTS With the addition of contact sports for girls such as ice hockey, wrestling, and rugby, coupled with the increasing levels of physicality amongst young women, will gender-based sports teams at high school eventually be eliminated? If young women can participate on a co-ed wrestling team, why not young men hitting the floor mat in rhythmic gymnastics or the pool for synchronized swimming?

GERM FACTORY This is another name for an elementary school; *see Occupational Hazards (b), Sick Days, Sneeze, Vacation (2).*

GIFTED What many parents believe their child to be, despite overwhelming evidence to the contrary; *see Einstein, Intelligence Quotient.*

GLOBE This spherical piece of equipment is found in many classrooms. If the globe refuses to spin and still includes Yugoslavia and the Union of Soviet Socialist Republics, the teacher should consider just how useful an instructional tool it really is outside of History class. More contemporary versions are often available at reasonable prices at garage sales.

GOLF TEAM This is the best coaching assignment in a high school since the teacher gets to play a round of golf for free on a work day. Playing with student team members is not as dangerous as football, as embarrassing as basketball, or as foolhardy as cheerleading; *see Volunteer Labor, X-Treme Sports.*

GOSSIP This is the life blood of any school. Innovations may come and go, the principal may be transferred, and edubabble can be difficult to understand. Gossip on the other hand, is constant, and the bottomless pit of potential material keeps it forever fresh. The "news" is almost always easy to comprehend. If the scuttlebutt is garbled or incomplete, alternate information can be added to provide zest to the story; *see Grapevine, Office Reception Area (b), Shop Talk, Watering Hole.*

GOTH LOOK While most would agree that a teacher should be hired solely on ability, there are limits. A prospective teacher who has not moved on from the Goth scene of the 1990's may have a difficult time finding employment despite solid instructional skills. Walking into the job interview wearing black pants, black shirt, black eyeliner, black nail polish, black dog collar, metallic chains, and sporting spiked, dyed black hair will ensure that the candidate stands out from the others vying to teach first grade. If by some miracle the person is the successful applicant it would be wise not to get hopes up regarding an imminent move to the principal's chair; *see Dress, Fads (Fashion), Job Interview, Jocks and Jockettes, Versace, Gucci, and Armani.*

GOVERNMENT FUNDING To make the math easier, assume a $10,000 government allocation per student, attending two hundred school days at five hours each day. Without including the volunteer teacher time coaching teams, directing theatrical productions, conducting musical productions, or sponsoring clubs, the system costs the taxpayer approximately ten dollars per hour. This is roughly the equivalent of the minimum wage levels found in several states; *see Education (Public), Societal Expectations, Volunteer Labor, Zeitgeist.*

GOVERNMENT INTERFERENCE Positive government interference in education rarely extends past sound bites and catchy sloganeering. These provide an impression of caring that can translate into votes on an election day. Negative interference, usually through budget cuts or tougher standards, gives the public an impression of the politician looking after precious taxpayer money and . . . well . . . being tough. Either way, the politician wins. Either way, the schools don't; *see Blame Industry, Dramatic Performance (c), Journalists, Jurisdiction, Politicians, Societal Expectations, Zig-Zag (b).*

GPA During a particularly active staff social, a teacher may erroneously believe GPA (Grade Point Average), to be a version of IPA (India Pale Ale), and assume GPA stands for German Pale Ale. This error may provide hints to the teacher's GPA in university, or the amount of IPA consumed during the night in question; *see Beer, IPA, Marking (a/c), Xmas Staff Parties.*

GRADE INFLATION There was a time when a C grade indicated average progress. Now, due to pressure from parents, principals, and post-secondary schools, a teacher who issues a C grade is indicating poor student progress. The letter grade indicating average work is now a B. If the trend continues, young teachers may see a time in their careers when an A is an average grade. Perhaps a system of plus signs could be added with comments such as; "Johnny will have to work much harder if he wants to bring this A++ mark up to the A++++ passing grade"; *see A (Letter Grade), Educational Correctness, Helicopter Parents, Honor Roll, Report Cards.*

GRADUATION A rite of passage in contemporary society, this event has much more to do with fashion, theater, elaborate pranks, and marketing hype than educational achievement. Given that many students have blended families with an army of relatives requiring tickets, the days of one grad-two guests have disappeared. Teachers organizing graduation ceremonies should book the local sports arena as most school gymnasiums will not be large enough to accommodate the crowd. There will be at least one uncomfortable scene as two parents scream and holler at one another, unable to contain their animosity despite their child's big event; *see Blended Families, Conflict -Parental, Graduation Inflation, Yearbook.*

GRADUATION INFLATION Completed Kindergarten? a graduation ceremony is in order. Finished elementary school? The triumph deserves a ceremonial send-off. Survived middle school? The success merits some form of congratulatory ceremony. Placed your name on a register for a final year of high school? The "achievement" must be rewarded with a lavish self-congratulatory evening akin to the Academy Awards; *see Grade Inflation, Graduation.*

GRAPEVINE This is the method and speed at which gossip travels. For the best impact, the message should spread via face-to-face encounters. That allows the "news" to be received with wide eyes, an open mouth, and a slack jaw. Given its low-tech nature, this communication conduit is surprisingly fast; *see Electronic Communication (2), Gossip, Watering Hole.*

GRISHAM, JOHN This author represents contemporary literature for the classroom, replacing Emmerson, Dickens, and Hardy. After all, how many books did those guys sell? *see Functional Literacy, Harlequin Romance, Relevance.*

GUEST SPEAKER NEGATIVITY In the past, university students were the audience for all manner of advocacy groups who were opposed to pretty much every aspect of society. These speakers have inched into high schools, urged on by activist teachers and their student acolytes. It is common to hear their thinly disguised propaganda as they blabber on to a captive audience of teenagers. Favorite topics can include two dystopian views of the same coin, such as; anti-globalization and anti-protectionism; anti-fossil fuel and anti-wind turbines; anti-gender stereotypes and anti-male testosterone; anti-high-rise housing and anti-low-rise housing, and so on . . . and the public wonders why depression and anxiety rates amongst adolescents are on a steep curve upward after listening to the anti-everything movement.

As the teachers return to classrooms to deal with the student reaction, the guest speaker departs in an SUV and heads to Starbucks. While consuming a low-fat latte and a chocolate muffin an internet search will commence for more material in which to lambaste the "system" at the next gig; *see Bias Over Balance, Qualifications (e).*

GUM In another era students chewing this treat occupied the top rung of miscreants. This offense has now been replaced by the consumption of illicit narcotics, weapons possession, and disturbing levels of violence; *see Emergency Preparedness, I Don't Know (Poor Responses-a), Notes in Class, Nurturing Environment, Safety Education, Weapons.*

GYM RATS These pesky creatures can be found at most middle and high schools and even in some elementary schools. They nest in the same space, day after day. They swagger about as if they own the place, which, in a way they do. They cruelly repel library bookworms and theater nerds who wander into their territory. They connect with the Physical Education teachers while treating other instructors with benign disinterest.

H

HABITS Personal idiosyncrasies will be what adolescent students remember most about a teacher. Temper displays, favored phrases, clothing worn, necklaces tugged, earrings pulled, and keys jingled will all be remembered by students in minute detail long after any hoped-for gain in knowledge or skills has been forgotten; *see Dress, Fads (Fashion), Mean.*

HALLOWEEN This stimulant festival for children causes sugar-induced hyperactivity in elementary students for at least one week after the event. If a school organizes a dress-up day, several children will tumble into the dirt and ruin their costumes. Others will rip the clothing on a sharp edge. Peanut butter may be wiped on princess dresses and cola spilled on cowboy chaps. Tiaras and hats will be left on desks and tables, soon forgotten and suddenly missed. A horde of teary-eyed children will be roaming the school, making a mockery of the fun-day moniker; *see Unforeseen Consequences.*

HALLWAY CONVERSATIONS Ironically one of the best places for teachers to engage in a private conversation is in the hallway when a high school or middle school is changing classes. The packed corridor is crammed with adolescents, talking, gawking, poking, groping, laughing, or sobbing. The students are so engaged at being the epicenter of their own universe that any conversing teachers are virtually invisible; *Dramatic Performances (b), Middle School.*

HALO A shimmer of goodness and light, this is immediately worn by the most disruptive student in the class when disturbances cause the teacher to look up and search for a likely candidate to reprimand. These students have high levels of premonition and timing; *see Classroom Management, Jason, Judge and Jury, Pareto Principle, UFO (1).*

HARD COPY What happened to the prediction of the paperless work place? Teachers can contemplate that infamous prognostication while waist high in printed copy courtesy of modern electronic communication. Never has sending memos from the school board office been so easy; type, click, and email a directive to print a copy for all employees. Piles of paper provide tangible evidence that central office bureaucrats are alive and well. The paper and ink costs could pay for additional supplies for students but that would interfere with adult-level information flow; *see Blended Families, Desk, Health and Safety, Insurance Investigations, Knee-Deep*

Syndrome, Laws of Bureaucracy (a/b), Non-Carbon Paper, Report Cards.

HARLEQUIN ROMANCE

1. This is contemporary literature best read during the summer in the privacy of a teacher's home; *see Educational Correctness, Functional Literacy, Grisham, Literature.*
2. Resembling a print version of daytime television, the romance novel has considerable potential to link with soap operas and reality TV in the design of new and relevant curriculum; *see Oprah, Relevance, Television, Television Screen.*

HARRY POTTER These tales are a relatively safe choice for a novel study, though a few extremely religious families may be opposed to the wizardry and sorcery. Of course, these same parents will also have issues with the Chronicles of Narnia, the Wizard of Oz, and Macbeth; *see Kipling, Novels.*

HAZE This is an apt descriptor of the thick air in staffrooms of a bygone era when not only was smoking permitted, the vast majority of teachers engaged in the vice with gusto. Crazy as it seems today, schools were not the only environments thick with cigarette smoke. People were allowed to smoke on airplanes and in movie theaters. Smoking in the staffroom seems so outlandish that it might be able to qualify for a comment in a *Ripley's Believe It Or Not* museum, especially if a photo of the teachers of yore satisfying their nicotine addiction could be provided for verification.

HEALTH AND SAFETY If the bottom twenty percent of a teacher's classroom wall space is covered in mold; if the air vent in the chemical storage room adjacent to the Science lab is blocked with plywood; if the toilet paper in the staff restroom runs out before recess; a health and safety report should be completed. You will likely have to inform the secretary who will tell the principal. The principal will provide fourteen forms to complete in triplicate. The paperwork will be forwarded to the maintenance department who will refer it to the human resources department who will contact the teachers' union. This process will take three months. Another two months will pass until the union's health and safety rep will chastise the member for not reporting the issue in a timely manner; *see Hard Copy, Non-Carbon Paper, Office Workers, Principal, Union/Association, Varnishing Room.*

HELICOPTER PARENTS Hovering above their children, these parents take their role as protector and guardian seriously; too seriously. An interesting challenge for educators is to devise an A-Z glossary describing the parent behavior which includes; advocating, bullying, cajoling, demeaning, excusing, fighting, gossiping, harassing and so on . . . already with eight letters complete! There are reasonable odds that their children will grow up to be emotionally stunted adults; *see A (Letter*

Grade), Bubble Wrap Kids, Fault Police, Grade Inflation, Honor Roll, Notes in Class.

HEROES AND HEROINES These teacher colleagues continually display acts of bravery, such as cleaning the staffroom coffee cups, giving up their spot in the microwave line, and diving into the bowels of a photocopier to fix a paper jam; *see Microwave, Mug, Xerox.*

HIDDEN CURRICULUM An outdated term, the concept referred to teachers being surreptitious role models by their choice of dress and deportment. The title indicates a process with less-than-desirable levels of transparency, at least by contemporary standards. This makes the idea's return to favor unlikely; *see Basketball, Quaint Ideas/Quaint Technology (1), Wise Sage.*

HISTORY The concept of history is a difficult one for young people. Students think two years ago was a long time in the past. Seventh-grade students can often be heard saying, "Way back when I was in the fifth grade." They see their parents as ancient (possibly from Da Vinci's time), and their teacher might be even older; *see Ethnocentrism.*

HOME SCHOOLING From a purely political point of view there is not much downside to this activity. Firstly, much like public funding for private schools, government support for the concept demonstrates flexibility by recognizing and respecting the individual needs of families. All politicians wish to be seen as being pro-family. Secondly, if five percent of the student population are home schooled, that is five percent that do not have to be accommodated in school buildings that require maintenance and be filled by teachers who need to be paid from the public purse. Within certain limits, home schooling is a rare political double-win. Few elected officials can resist such a splendid political opportunity; *see Government Funding, Politicians, Wits on Education.*

HONOR ROLL Since everyone in today's world needs to be rewarded in some fashion for the work they do, no matter how mediocre, the number of recognized students on these lists has more than quadrupled in the last few decades. There are Honor Rolls and Super Honor Rolls and Principal's Honor Lists and Effort Lists and Merit Lists and Try Harder Next Time Lists and so on. The shortest recognition roll of all would be the names of students not on any lists; *see A (Letter Grade), Grade Inflation, Helicopter Parents, Outstanding.*

HORMONES WITH FEET Brevity is the soul of wit. This description of early adolescent students is concise and accurate; *see Dramatic Performance (b), Eighth-Grade Boys, Kayaks and Canoes, Middle School, No Man's Land, Notes in Class, Seventh-Grade Girls.*

HOT DOG Formerly the gastronomic king of the fund-raising program, the dubious nutritional value has moved it into a distant second place behind a much more culinary correct, ethnically connected, flat-dough bread; *see Food Police (2), Lunch Sales, Nourishment, Pizza.*

HUMOR A sure sign of the onset of teacher burnout is the loss of a sense of humor. If a teacher feels it slipping away, borrow a copy of this book from a friend. Better yet, buy one; *see First- Year Teacher, Keener.*

I

IDIOMS Primary age children tend to take speech literally. If a high school teacher is suddenly thrust into the challenge of being in front of a group of second graders, nervousness is to be expected (and for good reason). Despite the anxiety, do not use idioms as these will cause confused consternation amongst the little ones. Five of the more common idioms to avoid are:

a) break a leg;
b) speak of the devil;
c) kill two birds with one stone;
d) when pigs fly;
e) hit the books;

see Fault Police.

I DON'T KNOW (GOOD RESPONSES) Difficult as it is, this statement is a good reply to certain student queries. Examples of questions to which "I don't know" is an appropriate response are:

a) "How do rabbits have so many bunnies?"

b) "Should I live with my mom or my dad?" *see Blended Families, Conflict (Parental);*
c) "Does the president always tell the truth?"

I DON'T KNOW (POOR RESPONSES) Teachers should not get carried away with the "I don't know" reply as on occasion it is not the best answer. Examples of student questions to which this response is not appropriate are;

a) "Why is the principal so mean?"
b) "Can you get me some beer for Friday night?" *see Beer;*
c) "Will you go out with me on Saturday night?" *see Ogling.*

I GENERATION Veteran and retired teachers may rue the supposed self-centeredness of millennial-aged teachers who were raised on iTunes playing on iPhones and who gawk at selfies on iPads. It is easy to forget that the veteran teacher and his or her baby boom buddies were labeled the "Me Generation" for displaying exactly the same traits; *see Apple Inc., Baby Boom Teachers, Techno-Gadgets.*

ILLICH, IVAN There are always a handful of loony ideas permeating education faculties. Perhaps none today can equal Ivan Illich's book, *Deschooling Society,* released in 1971. The publication was well regarded by many left-leaning education professors who considered Leon Trotsky a moderate wimp. This provides a good hint of the practicality of the ideas presented. Illich stated that, "Universal education through schooling is not feasible . . . Neither new attitudes of teachers toward their pupils, nor the proliferation of educational hardware or software, nor the attempt to expand the pedagogue's responsibility . . . will deliver universal education." *Deschooling Society* was required reading in a number of teacher-training programs. This put a comically impractical, negative spin on the students' future career choice. Worse, they were forced to pay for the "privilege" by forking out the cover price for the book and having their tuition fees fund the instructor to lead the discussion seminar; *see Education Professors.*

INFINITY It is difficult to teach a concept when you have absolutely no grasp of it yourself; *see Atlas, Intelligence Level.*

INFORMAL LEADER The student in a class with the most innate leadership skills is often the most talkative. Teachers can spend a great deal of time attempting to understand the traits that allow this student to sway his or her peers. Rarely is the leader the most studious and only occasionally is he or she the biggest or most attractive. Verbosity is clearly a factor as is a magnetic persona with a manipulating, almost malicious tinge. These students may eventually become politicians, mob bosses, or CEO`s of oil companies; *see Frankenstein, Number Fudgers, Rule Breakers (1), Self-Esteem (Student).*

INNOVATION A continuous circle that keeps people other than teachers employed. The process usually begins with announcements and fanfare followed by endless meetings which conclude with the decision to meet yet again. Workshops and seminars soon follow. A waiting period ensues to see what will happen. After a long delay, the next announcement will frequently contradict the first. The cycle will commence again. A teacher who takes no new action and waits long enough will return to the leading edge, at least for a time; *see Expert, Fads (Educational), Flip Flops (2), Leading Edge, Open Area Classrooms/Open Concept School, Principal (f), Workshops and Seminars, Zig-Zag (b).*

INQUIRY-BASED LEARNING Start with a question and then work to uncover the answer. Stripped down to its essence, this is inquiry-based learning. However, those proficient in edubabble demand that the idea is far more complex, rigorous, and robust than that. Only in education could professors write an entire book about such a topic, and conferences be dedicated solely to the issue. Only in education would people buy the book and pay to attend; *see Expert, Education Professors, Edubabble, Innovation, Leading Edge.*

INSTANT GRATIFICATION People expect to get what they want and they want it now. This may explain why so many adults are racking up credit card debt at a frightening rate. The attitudinal shift toward instant gratification is not only about acquiring tangible goods and the adults who purchase them. For many students there seems to be little point at working to master quadratic equations or ascertain the reasons underlying the war of 1812 if they are not gratified by immediate understanding. Having to spend more time and effort to receive any reward can seem so demeaning; *see Instant Response, Math for the Masses, Work Habits.*

INSTANT RESPONSE People expect an instant response and they want it now. This includes the parents, the principal, the janitor, the secretary, and the coffee fund collector. If not given an immediate answer they remind you via email until you are drowning in unmet expectations. Remember that no one really expects a person to reflect and think about an appropriate reply. Just shoot off any response into cyberspace and the vast majority of people will be satisfied that they were heard; *see Boss, Coffee Fund, Electronic Communication, Instant Gratification, Knee-Deep Syndrome, Tests (New Teacher).*

INSURANCE INVESTIGATIONS Being involved in one of these investigations is never enjoyable. Usually there has been a mishap of some sort. The teacher is at least partially involved or the investigator would not demand a meeting. Of course, the whole purpose is for the insurance company to pay as little money as possible, so the conversation may be cleverly steered in a particular direction. A teacher may be asked to verify any information by completing eleven forms in triplicate. Continuing the downward spiral into the bureaucratic nightmare is the possibility that once the insurance ordeal is over you will receive a phone call from a lawyer, or worse, a journalist; *see Fault Police, Hard Copy, Journalists, Laws of Bureaucracy (b), Non-Carbon Paper.*

INTELLIGENCE LEVEL A teacher may be proud to have a scholastic background that includes the completion of a university education. This accomplishment presumes at least a moderately above-average level of intelligence. However, given time and the number of students taught, teachers will inevitably instruct students brighter than they are, sometimes much more so. This can be ego-bruising despite the continuing teacher advantages of age, experience, and power. A reaction demonstrating intelligence and maturity is preferable to moping when realization hits that the teacher is, at best, the second smartest person in the class; *see Atlas, Infinity, Textbook (Teacher's Copy).*

INTELLIGENCE QUOTIENT This statistic is linked to a norm and is contradicted by the intense belief amongst virtually all parents that their child has an above average IQ. If this were true, almost all children would exceed the norm and a new definition of average would be required; *see Einstein, Gifted, Intelligence Level.*

INTERNET There is not much point in utilizing the old-fashioned, content-oriented "sage on the stage" instructional style when even the most dull-witted student can go online and within fifteen minutes gather at least as much content knowledge as what they would sitting and listening to the teacher's lecture. However, there is much "fake news" on the internet, not to mention outright lies. Learning to decipher the difference between factual truth and trumped-up fantasy is where students will need help. This is where teachers at middle and high school should focus, presuming of course, that they are able to discern the difference between internet-gathered fact and fiction; *see Orator, Relevance.*

INVESTMENT CLUB Dreaming of hitting the jackpot? A group of colleagues who regularly commit no more than five dollars per month in the hope of winning the lottery or hitting a home run on the stock market do. Regular payment is essential since there is a possibility that on an occasion when a staff member forgets to contribute, there will be an earth-shattering win. The unfortunate teacher will feel isolated amongst the hoopla as thirty ecstatic colleagues divide the one-hundred-dollar booty into equal amounts of $3.33; *see Back- to-School Sales, Dress, Lunch at a Restaurant, Wine.*

INVIGILATING This is one of the cushiest assignments for a high school teacher. During the formal examination schedule, the desks are aligned in long rows in the gymnasium. All the invigilator has to do is wander up and down the aisles with a serious look plastered across his or her face. The teacher is not allowed to answer any questions or provide academic assistance; the normal procedure being that he or she does not teach the subject being written. The only action that can interrupt this usually placid assignment is the fire alarm. Then all hell will break loose; *see Fire Drill, Jamming and Cramming.*

IPA India Pale Ale; *see GPA.*

J

JAMMING AND CRAMMING Despite initial appearance, this entry has nothing to do with impromptu music sessions or last-minute studying for exams. The unpleasant circumstance referred to occurs most often in high schools as ten classes attempt to use one door for entry to an assembly, or one exit during an emergency drill. This makes the hall leading to the door resemble a Los Angeles freeway, and only marginally safer. While this logjam may not be of much concern during a practice drill, envisioning the crush of teens during a real emergency with the teacher imploring them to remain calm does not make for a restful sleep; *see Assembly, Emergency Preparedness, Fire Drill, Invigilating.*

JANITOR As the school's chief operational officer, this person shares top billing with the head secretary. With the power to allocate keys, desks, and file cabinets, this is a person to have onside. Once a positive relationship is established the classroom will be clean and largesse will flow; *see Desk. Filing Cabinet, Fruit Flies, Gum, Keys, Office Workers, Oranges, Vice-Principal.*

JASON A once-popular student name chosen by middle class parents; a teacher could have had as many as five of these in a class, all displaying remarkably similar obnoxious behavior; *see Classroom Management, Halo, Judge and Jury, Pareto Principle, Untruthful Statements.*

JAVA Many teachers are addicted to this stimulant which is readily available in the staffroom. There is usually a need for two shots in the morning before class and another at recess despite the dreadful product quality; *see Coffee Machine, Teachers' High, Mug, Occupational Hazards (d), Recess, Valium, Veteran Teachers (d).*

JAZZY PRESENTATIONS There is a direct though inverse correlation between hyped-up, gaudy, techno-driven presentations and the quality of the information, opinion, or analysis provided. The medium used is far more important than the message; *see Number Crunchers, Power Point, Relevance, Techno-Gadgets, Workshops and Seminars.*

JEANS Despite the cost, especially when compared to more common teacher attire, this clothing can be irrationally regarded as too casual for teaching. If jeans are worn, they should not be tight (too controversial), flared (too disco), or frayed (too 1960's). Those who aspire to snob status should consider designer labels; *see*

Dress, Fads (Fashion), Jocks and Jockettes, Versace, Gucci, and Armani.

JIVE DANCING At one time considered scandalous, this form of gyration can only be described as dull on the lewd meter when compared to the moves made by many students at high school dances. Contemporary "dancing" often leaves little doubt about desire or intent; *see Dance (1).*

JOB AD Be careful! When a far-flung school district is desperate for teachers all manner of promises can, and are, made. The school, the students, the equipment, the supplies, and the job perks may bear little or no resemblance to the statements made in the glossy spread of the recruitment ad. If there are six vacancies on a seven-member staff and the lone returnee is the principal, the odds are good that there is something amiss; *see Job Interview.*

JOB INTERVIEW One of the few occasions when teachers are expected to engage in hyperbole and unabashed self-promotion, the candidates usually fall into one of the following groups:

a) those that are embarrassed by such boasting and perform poorly at the interview;
b) those who lean to narcissism and love talking about themselves and how proficient a teacher they are; *see Yappers (2);*

c) those that are excellent teachers yet cannot describe exactly what they do, much like Michael Jordan trying to explain split second decisions on the basketball court;

d) those who have no idea what they are talking about and attempt to bafflegab and edubabble their way through the process; *see Curriculum Coordinators, Edubabble, Expert;*

see Goth Look.

JOB INTERVIEW (RESPONSES) At the conclusion of an interview, the candidate will likely be given an opportunity to ask one or two questions. A few that should be avoided are:

a) "What are your qualifications for the job?" directed to the principal;

b) "Why is the pay in this school district so much lower than in others?"

c) "Can I advertise my online business on the school's website?"

JOCKS AND JOCKETTES This sartorial style is *de rigueur* for elementary school teachers despite body type and regularity, or lack thereof, of an exercise regimen. The most popular examples are running shoes, polo shirts, and combination athletic suits of jackets and sweat pants in the brightest colors imaginable. Eschewing old-fashioned cotton; velour, fleece, and stretch-nylon are popular fabric choices; *see Dress, Fads (Fashion), Goth Look, Jeans, Versace, Gucci, and Armani.*

JOKES Unless a teacher is particularly fond of harassment accusations or poisoned workplace charges, avoid telling wisecracks and witticisms in the staffroom. After all, when sex, gender, profanity, stupidity, sexual orientation, and physical size are removed from jokes, there is not much left to work with; *see Educational Correctness, Testosterone Poisoning, Workplace Poisoning.*

JOURNALISTS Contact from one of these "professionals" will usually cause a teacher's heart to pump faster and perspiration to ooze from a worried brow. There is good reason for this. The teacher is going to pay, not monetarily as when engaging with a lawyer, but in some other painful manner. The journalist on the other end of the email or telephone line is solely motivated by meeting the story deadline with a nice juicy quote from the teacher. It is probable that you, your colleagues, the school, or teachers-in-general will not be cast in a favorable light in the local newspaper. In the internet era fewer people read these publications and the public scathing of the teacher, school, or education system may be more intense on Twitter; *see Blame Industry, Fault Police, Insurance Investigations, Self-Esteem (Teacher).*

JUDGE AND JURY As several lawyers have argued in court across the United States, students do not leave their civil rights at the front entrance of the school. Intervening in unending childhood and youth disputes, the teacher performs the role of police by questioning suspect(s); represents the jury, by determining guilt or innocence; and acts as the judge, by issuing a sentence. And who said teaching was boring or a teacher powerless? *see Classroom Management, Duty, Halo, Jason, Teacher, UFO (1), Untruthful Statements, Yarn.*

JUNGLE (BLACKBOARD) This is a film classic for teachers and they are strongly advised to watch the old movie at least once. If a teacher's work situation is similar to that portrayed in the movie, the teacher should be able to:

a) directly relate to the scenes as if watching yourself at work more than sixty years ago; *see Gum, Safety Education;*

b) feel good that the negative student behavior in a classroom today is not much different than it was in the 1950's.

If the teacher's work situation is worse than that portrayed in the movie, consider filming your class and school, writing an outline for a screenplay, and sending it to a movie producer who specializes in churning out B-level horror movies; *see Movies About Teachers.*

JURISDICTION The jurisdictional pie in education is finite and the number of power-hungry people and organizations demanding a bigger slice is increasing. Resembling animals visiting an ever-diminishing watering hole, the organizations eye each other warily. Any gluttonous grab for more pie results in less for the others. The tug can be formal, such as the government's role as opposed to the local school board, or the district's principals vis-a-vis the superintendent. The tussle can be at the school level, between parent politicos and the school staff; or broad based, with the teachers' union or association vis-a-vis pretty much everyone; *see Division (c), Government Interference, Parent Council (c), Politicos, Principal (f), School Board Members, Union/Association.*

K

K This term is popular in techno-speak, a language combining gibberish with English. People usually forget that K refers to memory; *see Techno-Geek.*

KAFKAESQUE Relatively few teachers are familiar with Franz Kafka, despite the author being generally regarded as one of the key literary figures of the twentieth century. A Miriam-Webster definition of Kafkaesque is, "Relating to or suggestive of Franz Kafka or his writings, especially having a nightmarishly complex, bizarre, or illogical quality." Is there any more accurate description for the stifling educational bureaucracy? *see Education Professors, Government Interference.*

KALEIDOSCOPE This word has varying significance to specific groups of teachers. Elementary teachers think of the importance of primary colors. Art teachers believe the term to be a good introduction to color theory.

Retired teachers, if they have any memory of the era, think about the 1960's; *see Baby Boom Teachers, Yellow.*

KAYAKS AND CANOES Any outdoor education field trip is a precarious adventure, especially one on flowing water with early adolescents attempting to handle a kayak or canoe. Student whining will not take long to surface, especially from individuals who possess muscle tone resembling jelly caused by sitting in front of a computer screen all day. For them, any physical activity is foreign. There will also be a number of clumsy students who will have difficulty putting on a life-jacket. A few others will chafe at wearing one, considering it to be a fashion disaster. The more physical students will be too active, wielding their paddles to smack classmates on the buttocks. After the first thirty minutes of the three-hour trip, the teacher will need to stifle the urge to send the most vociferous whiners on a wrong turn in the river that leads to class five white-water rapids; *see Camping, Field Trips (b), Hormones With Feet, Middle School, No Man's Land.*

KEENER Hopping on and off every educational bandwagon moving along the roadway and volunteering to serve on every school committee, this high-energy teacher may be heading for a hard fall. A teaching career is a marathon rather than a sprint; *see First-Year Teacher, Innovation, Professional Learning Community, Veteran Teachers.*

KEYNOTE SPEAKER Under certain conditions, a teacher should not feel guilty about missing the speech that opens a conference. After all, many business leaders skip the keynote, preferring to do real work like closing deals in the hotel bar. If there is a positive response to at least one of the following questions, a troubled teacher conscience can be assuaged and the individual praised for the truancy:

a) Has the speaker worked outside a public school for at least five years? *see Expert;*

b) Does the speaker use props such as puppets?

c) Does the speaker read directly from the power point slides assuming attendees to be illiterate? *see Education Professors, Jazzy Presentations, Power Point, Techno-Gadgets.*

KEYS Possessing these low-tech gadgets puts a teacher higher on the status ladder than most students, who have to wait at locked doors before entering a room. Before boasting about an exalted place in the hierarchy, note that the janitor frequently flaunts a truly impressive set of keys on a belt buckle; *see Filing Cabinet, Janitor.*

KIDS This term can be interspersed with "children" or "boys and girls" at elementary school. Avoid using the above terms when describing high school students who can become quite annoyed when being referred to as children. When speaking to adolescents, stick to "kids" or the more formal "students." More colorful descriptive language of various teenage miscreants should be saved for the watering hole or private conversations with your kindred spirit; *see Kindred Spirit, Shop Talk, Watering Hole.*

KINDERGARTEN STUDENTS It is not surprising that Kindergarten children can experience separation anxiety in the first month or two of the school year. School is a foreign environment, much bigger and noisier than home. From a child's perspective, the adult taking the place of the parent, while kind, does not provide much food. The child cannot call this adult, "mom" or "dad", and is forced to use a much longer title instead, such as "Mrs. McGilligutty" or "Ms. Shoenbrauner." Names like these are tough to pronounce for the average five-year-old child. Kindergarten children must wonder why they are taken to this strange, big building to play when they could easily do so at home; *see Kindergarten Testing.*

KINDERGARTEN TEACHER This special breed of teacher is similar to a mother wolf caring for a pack of cubs; passive, nurturing, and easy to cuddle. Caution should be exercised when the safety of the cubs is threatened as the normally placid persona is replaced by howling, snarling, and other aggressive behavior; *see Altruism, Zealot.*

KINDERGARTEN TESTING While not understanding the term laboratory, perceptive Kindergarten children may regard the strange place called school as some sort of testing facility. In the first month of attendance various unknown adults wearing white coats will poke and prod them with needles and shine bright lights in their ears and eyes; *see Kindergarten Students.*

KINDRED SPIRIT Not having this type of colleague is lonely. Having more than two is a clique. One should be cautious when all conversation between you is "shop talk" and you begin wearing identical work clothes; *see Dress, Jock and Jockettes, Shop Talk, Watering Hole.*

KING KONG At least a few times in a career a teacher will encounter a male student who resembles the famous primate; big, kind-hearted, misunderstood, and, if you are a female teacher, enamored with you. It is wise to be nice, but not too nice, to these students; *see Lingerie.*

KINGS AND QUEENS Despite the oft-mentioned myth, there is no guarantee that teachers work well together. This does not imply that they could not do so effectively, it simply means that compared to other adults, they rarely have the opportunity. They spend the day with students, ruling over classrooms that are not operated democratically. While most teachers may be benevolent despots, they are despots nonetheless; kings and queens in their own classroom who are used to getting their way the vast majority of the working day. This may explain why it is so difficult to convince teaching staffs to join each other in one boat, never mind having them row in the same direction; *see Brainstorming,*

Conservative-Thinking Liberals, Cooperative Learning, Mission Statement, Principal (e).

KIPLING, RUDYARD A British imperialist and therefore not politically correct, little of this author's work, despite the quality, is used in classrooms. Other authors who eventually may meet the same fate include:

a) Charles Dickens, who wrote about wealth disparity in Victorian England, causing some to believe his work to have a socialist tinge, thus annoying capitalist-loving conservatives;
b) Ernest Hemingway, who loved bullfighting, thus infuriating animal rights activists;
c) William Shakespeare, whose plays were performed by all-male casts at the Globe Theater (including boys playing the female roles), thus causing consternation amongst members of the feminist movement;
d) Mark Twain, who, despite his protestations that the novels *Tom Sawyer* and *Huckleberry Finn* were satirically anti-racist, included a plethora of racial slurs and stereotyping, especially in the latter novel, thus angering contemporary activists arguing for racial equality;

see Educational Correctness, Harry Potter, Novels.

KITCHEN KNIVES There are usually one or two large knives in the staffroom that qualify as weapons under school district policy. Use these with caution, not because of the sharp edges, but for the caked-on film covering the blade. It was once mayonnaise, mustard, or icing from the birthday cake consumed two months previously; *see Heroes and Heroines, Mug.*

KNEE-DEEP SYNDROME This state of being lasts from the beginning of the school year to the end. A common symptom is a tilted gait from lugging home a bag or briefcase stuffed with paper and sore, red eyes from reading the material. A psychological tendency to procrastinate often leads to a holiday filled with catch-up marking; *see Altruism, Desk, Multi-Tasking, New School Year Resolutions.*

KUNG FU Movies and television can stimulate playground activity. The relatively recent popularity of the *Kung Fu Panda* movies has led to much practice on the playground. This has caused teachers on duty to hope Hollywood produces more passive children's fare, though the days of *Cinderella, Mickey Mouse,* and *Sleeping Beauty* are long past; *see Duty, Playground Spats, X-Box.*

L

LATIN This language had no relevance for the vast majority of students and was finally dropped from the course offerings of most schools over one hundred years later than it should have been. Admiration should be extended to the common-sense educator who advocated that a subject be removed from a program of study. Such action is usually only initiated when the subject enrolment has dwindled to minuscule numbers as students "vote with their feet." Free-market course selection can cause anxiety amongst certain teachers. After all, at some point in time the subject they teach may meet the same fate as the previously essential Latin; *see Art, Curriculum, Frills, Relevance, Trophy Case (Sports).*

LAWS OF BUREACRACY Teachers know too well the traits of the education bureaucracy. They may take heart in that the education system is relatively "minor league" when compared to government, as the following "laws" may attest:

a) "In a bureaucracy, accomplishment is inversely proportional to the volume of paper used"; Fowler's Law; *see Hard Copy, Non-Carbon Paper;*
b) "If anything can go wrong, it will do so in triplicate"; Murphy's Law of Government; *see Hard Copy, Insurance Investigations, Non-Carbon Paper;*
c) "Never use one word when a dozen will suffice"; Smith's Principles of Bureaucratic Tinkering; *see Curriculum Coordinators, Edubabble, Expert, Politicos, Professional Learning Community, Psychobabble, Yappers (2);*
d) "A committee is twelve men doing the work of one"; veteran United States Senator, Edward "Ted" Kennedy; *see Camel.*

LEADERSHIP BULL It is understandable that one may believe this statement describes the questionable verity that emanates from the principal's mouth. This verbal mangling of the truth is certainly a topic worthy of humor, but not in this entry. The title above refers to a style of school leadership that is best described as a "bull in a china shop," with literary license to include male and female leaders. The bull method is relatively straight forward; lower head, go fast, run hard, snort a great deal, and trample any obstacle blocking the way. It may not be subtle, but it can be effective for brief periods of time. Unfortunately for the leader-bull, all that charging, snorting, and pawing demonstratively can get a little tiring. The teachers draw courage and lose their fear of being gored. They learn to step out of the way and allow the bull to barrel through, destroying not much else but air. After a time, the teachers become so used to the bull they barely notice the presence as the snorting behemoth is reduced to white noise; *see Dramatic Performance (c).*

LEADING EDGE More edubabble, the phrase is also known as cutting edge and is closely related to terms such as vanguard, lighthouse, and visionary. The proponents are almost always non-teachers, providing a significant clue as to the practicality of the proposed ideas. The life span of such innovative thought is roughly equivalent to that of a pop music group for the nine-to-twelve-year-old crowd; *see Edubabble, Expert, Flip Flops (2), Innovation, Inquiry-Based Learning, Open Area Classrooms/Open Concept School, Principal (f), Zig-Zag (b).*

LEARNED HELPLESSNESS Resembling adults who "use" the societal support system, a few enterprising special education students have perfected the technique of learned helplessness. A contributing factor is often over-zealous adult aides. For years they have pulled out the supplies for the student, spread them on the desk, and written the student's name on the assignment to "get them started." As the pattern became the norm one wonders who was training whom? Over the years the student has not learned much except manipulation and helplessness; *see Aides.*

LEARNING ASSISTANCE TEACHER A prime example of edubabble, this is a specially trained teacher for students experiencing learning difficulties. By definition, these teachers assist students to learn, leaving one to ponder the mandate of those teaching in the regular classroom; *see Abbreviations, Authentic Assessment, Professional Learning Community.*

LEARNING AT THEIR OWN PACE This is an oft-heard phrase describing individualized student learning. Why teachers listen to such meaningless edubabble remains a mystery. After careful consideration one would wonder at whom else's pace would a student learn? *see Authentic Assessment, Learning Assistance Teacher, Whole Language Approach.*

LEARNING SUITE The era of substantive, interactive, quality electronic learning packages in a whole range of subject areas has arrived. Prognosticators now ponder the future of teachers. All manner of interactive software can be tailored to individual student need. The software and hardware have other advantages; they are less expensive than teacher salaries, they don't take coffee or lunch breaks, and they don't go on strike, (at least not as yet); *see Illich, Names and Titles (e).*

LESSON PLANS Though fastidious planning is a brave attempt to put order into an otherwise chaotic environment, a teacher cannot adequately take into account all the variables that can destroy a carefully crafted plan such as:

a) fire drills and other emergency preparedness activities; *see Emergency Preparedness, Fire Drills;*
b) knocks at the door from the counselor, the principal, the vice-principal, or a parent; *see Zig-Zag (c);*
c) announcements over the public-address system; *see Office Workers, Principal, Zig-Zag (c);*
d) noisy students in the adjacent hallway;
e) disruptive students in the class; *see Halo, Jason;*
f) the lure of techno-gadgets; *see Fidget, Techno-Gadgets, Zig-Zag (c);*
g) special events such as an assemblies, dress-up days and dances; *see Assembly;*
h) Halloween (a week before and after), and upcoming holidays; *see Halloween.*

Good luck finding time to teach!

LIBRARIAN With no marking, no report cards, no regular classes, and no parent conferences, it is surprising that this colleague is considered a teacher. A weary classroom teacher may wish to ponder how to be assigned to the position; *see Counselors, Library.*

LIBRARY The central hub of the educational enterprise often located at the far end of the school. It is unlikely that a name alteration to 'Learning Commons" will mean much to students (though it will keep a few Education professors busy analyzing the impact). As with all education roles, the positive qualities of the personnel have a much greater impact on student learning than facility names or job titles; *see Librarian, Names and Titles.*

LINGERIE No matter how proud a teacher is of this item of clothing, or the parts of the body that it covers, it is well advised to keep these garments hidden, both in class and at the staff social; *see Beer, Dense (c), King Kong, Wine.*

LINOLEUM This is the flooring of choice for schools, usually in the dullest, most visually unattractive colors imaginable; *see Design, Wax.*

LITERATURE The educated adult, including, one would presume, teachers, used to be cognizant about literature. Now a person will have to look very hard, and be very lucky, to find youthful colleagues reading anything but mysteries, science fiction, entertainment magazines, and romance novels. Reading print novels only occurs on the few occasions when young teachers can be pulled away from their techno-gadgets and computer screens; *see Grisham, Harlequin Romance (1), Novels, Techno-Gadgets.*

LOGOS Nicknames that are politically, ethnically, or educationally incorrect are stirring controversy. So too, are school logos. A school may have a relatively common nickname such as Raiders. But if the logo features a big, muscular, half-naked male warrior with sword-in-hand, crushing a tiny-bodied defenseless opponent with blood oozing from a gaping injury, it is likely a few complaints will eventually find their way to the local newspaper; *see Journalists, Nicknames (Schools).*

LOL (LAUGH OUT LOUD) This is an excellent example of human creativity; techno-spelling shorthand necessitated by the limitations of technology and the attention span of many young people in the technological age; *see Bias Over Balance, Fidget, Techno-Gadgets.*

LUNCH AT A RESTAURANT This rare treat is reserved for professional development days. A group of teacher colleagues will spend ten minutes ordering, ten minutes eating, and twenty minutes discussing the bill, ensuring that the tip will not exceed more than eight percent; *see Dress, Investment Club.*

LUNCH SALES Hungry students require a lunch and many schools provide a program of hot lunches (pizza or hot dogs), dairy products (ice cream bars), or vending machine staples such as potato chips and pop. After lunch many students will attend lessons on the importance of proper nutrition; *see Advertising, Field Trips(c), Food Police, (2) Hot Dogs, Nourishment, Pizza.*

LYING *see Untruthful Statements.*

M

MARKETING This subject, along with data analysis and memo writing, is a new and important component of principal training programs, replacing outdated topics such as curriculum and leadership; *see Academy, Advertising, Data-Driven Decision Making, Football Team, Memo, Recruiting, Voucher System.*

MARKING Not many teachers enjoy this task. Tempting as it may be to stray from the traditional pursuit of assessing student work in solitary quietude, it is best to remain in the acceptable comfort zone. To be avoided are the following:

a) consuming a significant level of alcohol prior to reading student work. This may result in scathing written comments, or having student work ruined by beer sloshing from a fallen bottle; *see Beer, GPA, Neuron Forest, Wine;*

b) throwing the student assignments down the stairs and awarding the best grade to those that land at the bottom (or for variety, the top);
c) taking the student work to be marked on a weekend camping trip with your bowling buddies on the ludicrous premise that time and attention will be devoted to the task; not to mention risking the work being used as a starter for the campfire;
d) leaving the pile of student work to be marked beside a to-be-cleaned cat litter box in the garage.

MATH FOR THE MASSES There is a need to teach Calculus and Algebra. It is desirable that a bridge span covers the entire distance required, or that a capsule successfully rendezvous with the space station since a miss would mean a very long journey with not much to look at. But most people do not work in occupations such as structural engineering or astrophysics. The reality is that many students lack basic comprehension of Arithmetic. So too, do their parents who seem to believe that the difference between their credit card limit and the amount charged is "free" money. Concepts such as interest charges and percentage savings at a store are as confusing as reading Greek. Perhaps that is why the "roll back" prices at Wal Mart are noted in dollars and cents as opposed to a percentage; *see Division (a), Dyscalculia, Instant Gratification, Relevance.*

MEAN

1. The average class score on various tests, this result can be depressingly low despite a superhuman effort on the part of the teacher.
2. Some elementary students use this descriptor when discussing their teacher's personality. High school students display their increasing lexicon by using more colorful phrases and terms; *see Notes in Class, Uber-Planner, Ultimatum.*

MEDIAN Many teachers never understood the difference between mean and median when in university. Now, fully employed, it really does not matter; *see Dyscalculia, Standard Deviation, Zero (c).*

MEDICAL EXCUSE (PHYSICAL EDUCATION) There are many legitimate reasons for students to be medically excused from Physical Education class. Alas, there are several illegitimate reasons as well. These are usually concocted with parental support by sluggish, torpid students who are most in need of exercise.

MEDS This abbreviated version of medications has a less serious tone. High school students are responsible for taking their doctor-prescribed drugs. They may also choose to self-medicate with a few peer-prescribed varieties as well. In elementary schools, the responsibility for drug distribution often falls to the clerical staff. They dole out all manner of pills to eagerly awaiting children, usually just before recess or lunch. At these times their work space bears a closer resemblance to a medical dispensary than a school office; *see Office Reception Area (c), Office Workers.*

MEMO Professors of educational administration have apparently convinced prospective principals that the quantity of memo production equates to administrative competence. In an era of electronic communication even the most dim-witted administrator can pass this litmus test. Administrative notices may be contradictory. While the message may demand immediate attention do not leap into compliance. Wait for a day or two. The odds are good that a subsequent memo requiring different action will be forthcoming; *see Electronic Communication, Instant Response, Knee-Deep Syndrome, Open Door Policy, Principal, (a-f).*

MERCATOR PROJECTION This is one of the most common wall maps. The type of projection utilized gives the illusion that Canada is far larger than the United States. The actual territorial difference is not substantive, with Canada at 3.855 million square miles to 3.797 for the United States (3.16 without Alaska, which, like Canada, is similarly distorted). If a teacher is able to successfully explain the reason behind the visual distortion to students under the age of sixteen as well as to a few geographically-challenged colleagues, master teacher status should be bestowed; *see Atlas.*

MICROWAVE This staffroom appliance is in great demand at break times. The competitive nature of usually complacent teachers is revealed as they jostle for a prime spot in line. Colleagues who bring frozen food are quietly cursed; *see Food Police (1), Heroes and Heroines, Recess.*

MIDDLE SCHOOL Hyperactive, noisy, crazy, unpredictable, moody, peer-driven, and experimental; these words describe not only middle school students, but their teachers as well. How else could one survive a place that crams pre and early adolescents into one building for two or three years? Like a bizarre version of the Stockholm Syndrome, teachers first relate to, connect with, and then eventually become, adult versions of the kids who surround them; *see Dramatic Performance (b), Eighth-Grade Boys, Hallway Conversations, Hormones With Feet, Kayaks and Canoes, No Man's Land, Notes in Class, Seventh-Grade Girls.*

MIND MAPS On occasion a lesson goes too well and it is easy for a teacher to become energized, excited, and so enthused that it may be difficult to draw any conclusions from the session. A mind map can be a helpful instructional strategy as the visual representation of student comments promotes understanding. However, as students enthusiastically brainstorm for a half hour, the beaming teacher can get caught up in the action, offering unquestioning support by drawing circles, squares, triangles, and rectangles, before connecting them hither and yon with solid, dotted, and double lines. Not wishing to disrupt the flow of ideas, one, perhaps two, even three, whiteboards are crammed with a sprawling, muddled mind map. The teacher may attempt to conclude with a comment such as, "Okay, let's see what we've got," and proceed to stare incomprehensively at the jumbled swath of diagrammatic excess. A perplexed fifth-grade student may utter, 'I don't get it." At this point the teacher's best choice is to admit similar confusion and respond with, "I don't either."

MISSION STATEMENT If a parent committee worked to develop a statement reflecting the general idea of what the school's purpose should be, a reasonable consensus would likely be reached within an hour. If the task at a staff meeting is to translate that work into a mission statement, completion will take twenty times longer. The politicos, queen bees, opinion leaders, and yappers will debate every minute detail of word choice and punctuation; *see Brainstorming, Kings and Queens, Politicos, Principal (e), Quagmire, Queen Bee, Quest for Excellence, Yappers.*

MOVIES ABOUT TEACHERS Since educators so often receive verbal abuse from non-teaching friends and act as convenient scapegoats for the ills of society, it is understandable that movies that portray the profession in a positive light are popular with teachers. Though movies are illusory, they can still boost spirits and a teacher can dream of a reality that matches the on-screen fare. Frequent reactions to movies about teachers range from:

a) crying when watching the finale of *To Sir With Love* (for the sixth time);
b) cheering as the hero in *Teachers* stands steadfast against all odds;
c) longing for a send-off as portrayed in *Goodbye Mr. Chips;*
d) nodding knowingly about struggling to achieve a work-home balance as depicted in *Mr. Holland's Opus;*
e) laughing at the bumbling Arnold Schwarzenegger in *Kindergarten Cop.*

The Dead Poets Society, while a noteworthy teacher film, may be too dark for some sensitive teachers. They may better enjoy the ancient and anarchic *Carry On Teacher,* or the more modern *Bad Teacher* with Cameron Diaz; *see Jungle (Blackboard), Old TV Shows About Teachers, Songs About Teachers.*

MUG The container that is designed to hold a caffeine-laced stimulant is an employment necessity for many teachers. Strong bonds can develop between it and the owner. Mugs for visitors are rarely cleaned and the thick brown sludge that coats the bottom is impervious to knives, forks, and chisels. Despite this, visitor mugs are never thrown away and reside on the top shelf of a cupboard, awaiting the next luckless visitor/victim; *see Heroes and Heroines, Java, Kitchen Knives.*

MULTI-TASKING While wanting and needing four hands, six ears, and ten sets of eyes, a teacher will have to make do with the normal human allocation. Take heart, there are only twenty-five or more students to see at one time and only six questions to answer at once; *see Knee-Deep Syndrome, Questions (Student), Teacher, Umpire (Professional Baseball).*

MURALS Supposedly providing an attractive appearance to large blank expanses of hallway walls or exterior siding, murals are rarely removed. The permanence forces future generations to view the work that becomes quickly dated and often is of dubious artistic quality. Whatever personal view a teacher has of the project, it is wise to be positive and complimentary; *see Art, Educational Correctness.*

MUSICAL THEATER ROYALTIES Musicals such as *Oklahoma, Fiddler on the Roof, The Sound of Music,* and *The Wizard of Oz,* amongst others, are performed over and over and over again. The royalties are low, which is a significant factor for cash-strapped schools. An audience is virtually guaranteed. No matter how many times the parents have seen the old musicals, they will attend one, more or all performances if their son or daughter is in the show. Directors realize this and ensure that the cast is as large as possible; *see Volunteer Labor.*

N

NADIR Paradoxically those most engaged with providing instruction, teachers, are at the nadir of any influence on educational policy and reform. The adults with the most clout are the politicians, followed by education professors. School board members are next followed by parents, principals, and finally teachers. This list is a perfect inverse correlation; a person with most influence is the least engaged in the classroom; *see Education Professors, Expert, Government Interference, Occupational Hazards (g), Opinion, Politicians, Unforeseen Consequences.*

NAMES AND TITLES Several occupations have undergone name or title changes. The flight attendant moniker has replaced stewardess. Janitors are frequently referred to as custodians. Secretaries have become clerical staff and are occasionally called administrative assistants. Stock brokers are now financial planners. While teachers retain the traditional title, once the edubabble crowd focuses attention on the issue, the job name may change. A few with considerable potential are:

a) formal facilitators;
b) instructional interpreters;
c) learning leaders;
d) education engineers;
e) e-learning aides; *see Learning Suite.*

NAMES FOR SCHOOLS As with subdivisions, schools are often named for the natural environment that has been destroyed during construction. Thus, Meadow View Elementary occupies land that used to be a hillside meadow. Birch Creek High is so named for a creek that used to run through a former birch forest on the property. There are limits however. Few schools are tagged with names such as Swamp Land High or Gravel Pit Elementary; *see Academy.*

NANO-SECOND This approximates the amount of time it takes for a class to lose all decorum and civility in the teacher's absence. Multiply this number by ten to the ninth power to gauge the amount of time it will take to settle the students down; *see Classroom Management, Noise, Quiet Time, Television Screen, UFO (2).*

NEURON FOREST Apparently, people (yes, even students and principals), possess approximately one hundred billion neurons connecting at over one hundred trillion points, though it is doubtful anyone actually counted them. Being the owner of such an impressive forest makes a person feel more positive about doing a little logging after a long week in the classroom; *see Beer, GPA, Marking (a–d), Watering Hole, Wine, Xmas Staff Parties.*

NEW SCHOOL YEAR RESOLUTIONS Unlike the non-teaching population who make these promises in January, for teachers the year begins in September. Favorite resolutions are to stay on top of the marking load, to pay attention at staff meetings, and to refrain from gossip. The shelf life of such promises is usually no more than two weeks; *see Fidget, Gossip, Knee-Deep Syndrome.*

NICKNAMES (SCHOOLS) While professional sports teams are facing controversy over their nicknames (Washington Redskins, Chicago Black Hawks, Cleveland Indians), there are similar questions facing schools. Elementary school nicknames seldom offend, but high school monikers which highlight racial or ethnic groups may. The school could be caught in the middle of a battle between traditionalists who demand name retention, and members of the offended ethnic group who lobby for a change. Adding an adjective to the nickname, such as the Westview High "Friendly" Chiefs, or the Central High "Responsible" Warriors is not likely to be much help; *see Logos.*

NIMBY Not in my back yard (NIMBY), is a rarely admitted motivator by protestors given the decidedly selfish ring. However, it is the real impetus behind more than a few citizen rallies, usually concerning the location of power lines, homeless shelters, drug recovering centers, and correctional institutions being located in their neighborhood. School location can have a positive or negative impact on property values. Elementary schools in close proximity are normally regarded as positive by the residents. Nearby middle and high schools are as well, as long as they are not *too* close. No sane person wishes to have such an institution as a next-door neighbor; *see Names for Schools.*

NOISE Since students regularly watch television, plug-in on earphones, and work on school assignments simultaneously, they naturally see nothing wrong with talking, listening to music, and drumming on their desk while the teacher is at the front of the class trying to explain a concept that requires a modicum of thought and reflection; *see Classroom Management, Nano-Second, Non-Verbal Communication, Quiet Time, Ultimatum.*

NO MAN'S LAND What to do with those difficult hormone-intoxicated young adolescents and prepubescents too old for elementary school and too young for high school? place them in one institution and call it a middle school. Their teachers should receive twenty percent additional pay and a year-long sabbatical every five or six years to recover from battle fatigue; *see Dramatic Performance (b), Eighth-Grade Boys, Hormones*

With Feet, Kayaks and Canoes, Middle School, Notes in Class, Seventh-Grade Girls.

NON-CARBON (NCR) PAPER Occasionally the old methods are better. That must be the case as NCR paper is still used in some legal, insurance, and accident/injury cases where hard copy is required from the teacher. Be cautious! The odor from NCR paper can cause headaches and induce a mild "high", perhaps explaining the mood swings of some insurance investigators and lawyers. A wrist-strengthening regimen is necessary when working with forms that have four or more copies with warnings of "press firmly" written at the top. Non-carbon paper may make a comeback, if only because the phrase implies carbon reduction, a current hot-button environmental issue; *see Environmental Correctness, Hard Copy, Health and Safety, Insurance Investigations, Laws of Bureaucracy (a/b).*

NON-VERBAL COMMUNICATION This is a critical skill for controlling student behavior. A quick look can become a stare which can morph into an icy glare. For additional impact, gestures can accompany the eye contact such as scowling, putting hands on hips, or pointing a finger at the offending student. However, teachers should not be carried away with this form of communication. Techniques used in the past such as flinging chalk at students, smacking yardsticks on desk tops, and holding students in headlocks, effective as these may have been in indicating emotion, are frowned upon today; *see Chalk, Classroom Management, Electronic Communication (2), Grapevine, Jason, Nano-Second, Noise, UFO (2), Yappers (1).*

NOTES IN CLASS Young teachers will have difficulty believing that this was once a classroom management issue, particularly with hormone-ravaged, identity-seeking middle school students. Written notes were passed from student to student. Unrequited love and emoted loathing for one member of the opposite gender would often be written in a single note. Occasionally a teacher would snatch the message and threaten to read it aloud to the class. Some actually did, which would hardly be seen as appropriate by contemporary standards. In today's world the rotor blades of helicopter parents would be slicing the offending teacher in two the following day.

The written note has all but disappeared. Since pre and early adolescents are much the same as they always have been regarding affairs of the heart, a contemporary teacher can be assured that the thumb-tapped texts firing around cyberspace contain much the same content as what the students' parents and grandparents put to paper; *see Class Management, Dramatic Performance (b), Eighth-Grade Boys, Helicopter Parents, Hormones With Feet, Mean, Middle School, Seventh- Grade Girls, Texting.*

NOURISHMENT Maintaining stamina through a long teaching year is important and proper nourishment is required. Skip the potato-chip bags in the vending machines and opt for cheezies instead. Help meet the daily required intake of dairy products by using milk in your coffee. Talk the principal into using whole wheat buns for the hot dog sales to help meet wholegrain needs; *see Donuts, Food Police (1/2), Hot Dogs, Lunch Sales, Pizza.*

NOVELS Choosing a novel for study that doesn't offend at least one parent or student in a class is virtually impossible. A teacher can take the safe route and choose a novel with the least number of potential detractors, such as Harry Potter for the sixth or seventh grade. Or a teacher can throw caution to the wind and choose one that will offend almost everyone. The teacher can then drop the idea when the flack hits the fan and claim the actions to be educationally justifiable since the entire affair was concocted as an introduction to a unit on the right to protest. There is a slim chance that this strategy will work. It should only be used if the teacher has tenure and likes having his or her picture in the local newspaper; *see DVDs, Educational Correctness, Harry Potter, Journalists, Kipling.*

NUMBER CRUNCHERS Specializing in all things numeric, these measurement addicts examine raw data, correlate inputs to outputs, and derive fiscal frameworks through complex formula. Borrowing techniques and analysis from business, these people are gaining influence in education at the rate of something-squared, multiplied by something-cubed. Their efforts are similar to cramming square pegs into round holes; *see Accountability, Budget, Data-Driven Decision Making, Diving Into the Data, Number Fudgers, Quantification.*

NUMBER FUDGERS It is not surprising that when organizations and the people in them begin to live and die by numbers alone, there is a tendency to engage in a little tinkering. Massaging the numbers is common enough in the corporate world as a few former executives cooling their heels in prison can attest. Why not employ a similar strategy in education? *see Accountability, Benchmarking, Data-Driven Decision Making, Diving Into the Data, Frankenstein, Number Crunchers, Office Workers, Principal (d), Rule Breakers (1), Self Esteem (Student).*

NURTURING ENVIRONMENT This atmosphere, in which children learn best, is often readily apparent in elementary schools. It is still possible to achieve in high schools once the guns and knives have been removed; *see Emergency Preparedness, Gum, Weapons.*

O

OCCUPATIONAL HAZARDS There are hazards in every occupation and some of the more common ones faced during a teaching career are:

a) respiratory issues from spending a considerable amount of time in marginally clean classrooms; *see Carpeting;*

b) frequent colds and flu from germ-laden students spewing airborne viruses; *see Germ Factory, Sneeze, Vacation (2);*

c) thick skin on butts from sitting on cheap plastic chairs;

d) destroyed taste buds from drinking sludge-like coffee; *see Coffee Machine, Java;*

e) attention-deficit issues from too many long, rambling student and principal monologues; *see Fidget, Yarn;*

f) emotional fragility from receiving verbal shots from non-teacher friends about the length of vacation time and how "easy" teaching is; *see Boss, Knee-Deep Syndrome, Multi-Tasking, Teacher;*

g) reduced patience listening to non-teachers who know how to do your job better than you do; *see Boss, Education Professors, Expert, Innovation, Nadir, Opinion, Politicians.*

OFFICE RECEPTION AREA Non-class times are particularly busy. While the office staff plows on with their work, the following groups like to congregate:

a) for parent volunteers, a place to socialize;
b) for teachers, a place to snatch supplies and keep the rumor mill humming; *see Gossip, Grapevine;*
c) for elementary students, a place to receive first aid and drugs; *see Meds;*
d) for high school students, a place to sit sullenly and wait for the vice-principal; *see Vice-Principal;*

OFFICE WORKERS A combination first aid attendant, photocopy repairperson, answering service, front line defender, quartermaster in charge of supplies, IT specialist, and data manipulator for the principal, the office worker acts as the information hub of the school. Working in a cacophony of noise and responding to incessant demands from the educators, these workers know more about the school, the principal, the teachers, the support staff, and the swirling rumors about them than any teacher could imagine; *see Diving Into the Data, Gossip, Grapevine, Janitor, Meds, Office, Principal (c/d).*

OGLING This is an extremely poor behavioral trait in a teacher. Avoid such action, whether directed to students, student teachers, colleagues, secretaries, janitors, and parents. There is no such activity as covert ogling; you will be known and there are far better and more positive ways to develop a reputation; *see I Don't Know (Poor Responses-c), Jokes, Workplace Poisoning.*

OLD TV SHOWS ABOUT TEACHERS With the advent of numerous channels offering old-time TV it is possible for young and middle age teachers to be exposed to a sampling of ancient shows that featured teachers. A late 1960's, early 1970's dramedy, *Room 222,* stars an African-American History teacher with an inhumanly perfect level of understanding and patience. He is young, cool, and slightly anti-establishment, though the extent of his rebellious streak is laughable by today's standards. One of the more interesting sidelines is the presence of a young student teacher during the first several seasons. She must have been particularly incompetent given that she took at least three years to obtain her teaching license.

Less than a decade later the comedy *Welcome Back Kotter* hit the airwaves about an ex- "sweathog" student who returns to his old school to teach a new generation of his former ilk. Instead of being a vehicle for the actor playing Mr. Kotter, the show launched the rocket-ship career of John Travolta who plays Italian tough kid, Vinny Barbarino. Kotter must have been as incompetent as the student teacher on *Room 222.* The "sweathogs" seemed to take at least four TV seasons to finish their senior year; *see Movies About Teachers, Songs About Teachers.*

OLIGARCHY (LAW OF) No matter how democratically an organization commences, it will, according to this "law", eventually be dominated by a small cadre of people. Though the rule was devised long before the advent of most teachers' unions and associations, it accurately describes many aspects of their structure and operation; *see Politicos, Union/Association.*

ONE-HIT WONDERS There are a countless number of pop-music bands that are famous for one hit before failing to duplicate the feat. Desirous of boosting the relevance of literature, English teachers can link this fact to authors of a single famous novel who subsequently struggled to produce another successful work. An example of such writers could include Harper Lee, who only published one critically panned novel after *To Kill a Mockingbird.* J.D. Salinger became reclusive not long after *Catcher in the Rye* was published. Bram Stoker achieved more fame in his lifetime from working in the theater rather than writing *Dracula.* The marketplace can be a cruel master, a valuable lesson to students aspiring to conquer the business world; *see Grisham, Literature, Novels, Relevance, Voucher System.*

ONE-TRICK PONY One would think that with the variety of skills that teachers possess many could have been successful in alternate fields of employment. However, most teachers do not leave the school system for a different career, which has much to say about either their passion for the job, or the conservative, low-risk character traits they share. Flipping the career direction angle, it would be interesting to determine how many teachers entered the profession after a career in another field. This too, says may say much about how a teaching career is perceived by those outside education; *see Conservative-Thinking Liberals.*

OPEN AREA CLASSROOMS / OPEN SCHOOL CONCEPT In the lament of a maintenance department wit, "Walls come up, walls come down, walls go back up again." This statement was in response to the open area concept that hit American elementary education by storm in the 1970's. The bandwagon did not last long and the experiment withered and died, the spaces long-since converted into regular classrooms. The idea has returned, spouting similar benefits to the 1970's version, only this time being touted to include the entire school. Perhaps the "new" idea will catch on, perhaps it will not. One activity that will not happen is researchers surveying retired teachers who taught in open-area spaces to ascertain what went right and what went wrong; *see Baby Boom Teachers, Expert, Fads (Educational), Innovation, Leading Edge, Visionary.*

OPEN DOOR POLICY Principals are fond of using this phrase to describe their accessibility. This is only evident when they are not talking on the phone, doing paperwork, responding to emails, firing off memos, attending meetings, or disciplining students. These activities limit the principal to being truly accessible for no longer than ten minutes per day; *see Electronic Communication, Memo, Principal (a–f).*

OPINION There is no shortage of expressed opinions about public education in general and teachers in particular. One glance at some of the "person-on-the-street" interviews on local TV news reveals that contemporary society considers that everyone's opinion, no matter how ill-informed or ludicrous, is to be valued. This is a variation of, "Everyone has the right to an opinion," a cornerstone of a democracy. However, the phrase does not automatically confer that everyone's opinion is entitled to equal weight. Most people would defer to a surgeon's judgment about necessary medical intervention when compared to that of a stock broker. Similarly, a lawyer's view on the potential success of a criminal case would surely carry more weight than that of a welder. Common sense should indicate that a classroom teacher's opinion regarding public education would hold more sway than that of a taxi driver. Alas, common sense is not always as "common" as one may think; *see Expert, Nadir, Occupational Hazards (g), Politicians, Politicos.*

OPRAH How can a teacher possibly hold the attention of so many adolescent girls near the end of the school day when they are eagerly waiting to race home and watch Oprah? Try taping the show and using it as part of a current events unit; *see Hormones With Feet, Middle School, No Man's Land, Relevance, Television Screen, Wits on Education.*

ORANGES This is one of the most difficult fruits to eat without cutlery or plates and therefore one of the most popular in student lunches. Acidic juice sprays when being held too tightly during peeling, a fact not lost on some students who become adept at aiming the liquid toward others. After consumption there is usually a pool of juice on a desk, a chair, or the floor that turns to a sticky glue-like substance in a surprisingly short time. Avoid these areas and call the janitor who is trained, though not necessarily willing, to deal with the situation; *see Carpeting, Fruit Flies, Janitor, UFO (2).*

ORATOR The most dull, uninteresting colleague uses this teaching style, often accompanied by poor eyesight and hearing. Scant attention is paid to the student heads resting on desktops and gentle snores filling the room. However, on a positive note, this is one of the few teaching methods likely to achieve student silence; *see Internet, Quiet Time.*

ORCHID CHILDREN Occasionally the syndrome sloganeers miss an opportunity when a term is directly lifted from a language other than English. The descriptor for children who have a biological sensitivity to environmental context originates from the Swedish *orkidebarn*. Not only has the term avoided being labeled a syndrome, it may escape being linked with meaningless edubabble as well since there appears to be an authentic genetic-based causation for the trait.

OUTSTANDING This overused word describes slightly above-average talent and skill in students and colleagues. It also embellishes mediocre programs and marginally successful new teaching techniques. The gift for hyperbole does not rest solely with tabloid newspapers; *see A (Letter Grade), Grade Inflation, Honor Roll, Marketing, Principal (d).*

OVERHEAD PROJECTOR Once cutting-edge technology, it is difficult to locate one of these devices in today's schools. Other equipment meeting the same obsolete fate are Gestetners (a type of duplicating machine), and movie projectors (visual image players with a roll of film that wound through the machine from one exterior spool to another). Young teachers have difficulty believing such ridiculously cumbersome low-tech gadgets were once seen as important devices to support teacher work; *see Chalk, Pencil, Quaint Ideas/Quaint Technology (2), Techno-Gadgets, White-Out.*

OXYMORONS People are used to seeing oxymorons such as fresh-frozen, jumbo shrimp, or virtual reality in everyday life. Not surprisingly, edubabble contains a few gems as well. The "passive-aggressive" student may be assigned to the "advanced-beginner" class where the students watch “educational television” for most of the day. This enables the boy to eventually qualify for a “football scholarship”; *see Football Team, Television.*

P

PARENT COUNCIL Schools would not function well without parent volunteers, particularly at the elementary level. However, schools may function quite well without the council, whose effectiveness varies considerably from school to school. Impeding smooth functioning of any particular council are three types of destructive participants:

a) the single-focus parent supporting his or her offspring. If the child enjoys sports, the parent advocates for resources to be allocated to teams or gym equipment. If the child loves reading, the parent lobbies to increase the library budget. This tendency makes it difficult for these parents to objectively gauge the bigger picture of whole-school needs; *see Lunch Sales;*

b) the parent who brings a personal agenda to the parent council table, such as terminating the employment of the principal or a teacher. This makes it difficult for these parents to see any positive pictures; *see Boss;*

c) the politico parent who regards a leadership role on the parent council as a stepping stone to the political big time; the school board! This makes it difficult for these parents to see any picture beyond the upcoming election; *see School Board Members.*

PARETO PRINCIPLE This term is excellent example of edubabble. While sounding statistically complex it is easy to understand. Teachers see what the managerial principle describes every day and likely have more realistic insight. Borrowed from management and statistics, this analysis is based on the premise that not all inputs have the same or proportional impact on an output, often referred to as the 80/20 rule. Eighty percent of benefit can be achieved by twenty percent of the work, or conversely, eighty percent of the problems can be traced to twenty percent of the work.

Any teacher who has a few years of classroom experience knows this latter point applies to student behavior, though is likely to believe the 80/20 ratio is skewed. Removing one extremely unruly student from a twenty-five-member class (four percent), will result in more than eighty percent improvement in classroom tone. Vice-principals will attest to the same logic being applied across the entire school population; *see Classroom Management, Halo, Jason, Unidentified Flying Object (1), Vice-Principal.*

PAY SLIP

1. This piece of paper reveals a striking difference between the money a teacher earns and the amount allowed to keep.
2. The year-long statement of earnings for teachers, aides and even principals that is roughly the equivalent money to what an average major-league baseball player makes in one inning; *see Aides (a), Altruism, Teacher, Zealot.*

PENCIL The utility of this implement is like a spare tire for a car. You don't notice it until you need one. However, unlike the spare tire, which can usually be found, good luck to a teacher trying to locate a pencil. Even rifling through the secretary's desk is not likely to produce one. Colleagues either don't have one, or are unwilling to part with those they have, perhaps believing that scarcity will make them valuable one day. Asking a high school student for a pencil will draw a stare that combines wonder and confusion, mixed with a strong dose of pity; *see Chalk, Overhead Projector, Quaint Ideas/ Quaint Technology (2), Techno-Gadgets, White-Out.*

PENSION KNOWLDEGE Veteran teachers share the obsessive behavior traits of seventh and eighth-grade girls and boys. The world suddenly begins to look much different. Previously ignored monetary calculations, both their own and those of others, are important. The future looks different; *really* different. According to these teachers, even Mr. Garcia, the recently retired third-grade teacher, seems to have changed. At the risk of them eschewing political correctness, he looks a hell of a lot better than he did during his last year in the classroom. The brain keeps telling the tongue to talk incessantly about impending retirement. A previously forced smile is now a goofy grin.

Good luck to the young teacher trying to converse this obsessed human being; *see Eighth-Grade Boys, Seventh-Grade Girls, Veteran Teachers.*

PHONICS This method of teaching reading and language that has been lost in a sea of questionable innovation and edubabble. Pockets of teacher resistance remain and these rebels, operating in clandestine fashion, still use some of the teaching techniques; *see Educational Correctness, Renegades, Whole Language Approach.*

PIZZA Barging past hot dogs as the staple for lunch sales and fund raising, this dough-based pie has definite advantages:

a) it has an ethnic "feel." Hot dogs sound too domestic and can be equated with junk food; *see Field Trips (c), Food Police (1/2), Nourishment;*

b) it can contain at least a few vegetables. Though hot dog supporters claim mustard and relish to be vegetables, most people believe that argument to be a bit of a stretch; *see Food Police (2), Hot Dogs, Lunch Sales.*

PLAYGROUND SPATS Children appear to be incapable of solving issues on their own, thus requiring the intervention of an adult. In a past era the conflict was solved amongst the children, because if it wasn't, the game stopped, and nobody wanted that to happen. There appears to be a correlation between increased adult intervention and parental accusations of children's bullying behavior; *see Bullying Behavior, Duty, Excuses, Kung Fu.*

POLITICIANS These leaders are experts on all things related to teaching and education since they attended school in days gone by. This provides powerful insight and considerable vision which drives their commitment to eliminate the policies of their predecessors and launch their new improved version of educational reform; *see Blame Industry, Dramatic Performance (c), Expert, Government Interference, Jurisdiction, Innovation, Leading Edge, Nadir, Opinion, Testing (Standardized).*

POLITICOS Applying to a small minority of teachers, the term describes colleagues who live for the cut and thrust of union politics. Early in their careers they hone their verbal skills on the captive audience in the staffroom. To be most effective in defending teacher rights they pine for a full-time job with the union away from the classroom; *see Bias Over Balance, Jurisdiction, Laws of Bureaucracy (c), Oligarchy (Law of,) Opinion, Union/Association.*

POTENTIAL This is one of the most useful words a teacher can use to describe a student without saying anything substantive. All students have the potential to do or be something: an ambassador, a rocket scientist, or a brain surgeon. Conversely, the student may have the potential to be a successful thief, a corrupt official, or a sniper. The salient point for the teacher is not to elaborate. A simple, "He/she (insert name), has potential," is the optimum phrase. If pushed for more detail, try, "He/she (insert name), has the potential to do anything." This tactic is useful when speaking to lawyers during bitter child custody cases; *see Conflict (Parental).*

POWER POINT This nifty method of information delivery has led to a common affliction amongst presenters; the need to read every word flashed on the screen, presumably believing that the teacher audience has no more than a primary grade level of reading ability; *see Jazzy Presentations, Techno-Gadgets.*

PRINCIPAL A long career in teaching will likely mean working with an array of principals, some skilled and supportive, others weak-kneed and disorganized. Before rendering judgment on competence, it may be worthwhile considering the following:

a) the principal was not selected for his or her a high level of teaching ability, though the ability to talk about teaching was; *see Yappers (2);*
b) the principal used to be the boss. The position's authority has been steadily eroding for decades. A

teacher now has a myriad of bosses, the principal being only one of many; *see Boss;*

c) the principal spends more time working with the office staff than with teachers; *see Office Workers;*

d) the principal's word about school performance is rarely taken at face value since the outrageous hyperbole of years past has taken its toll on credibility. The principal is now required to provide statistical proof of his/her claims, rather than launching a long-winded, self-promoting speech; *see Diving Into the Data, Fidget, Office Workers, Outstanding;*

e) the principal supposedly leads and monitors teachers who are not the easiest people to supervise; *see Brainstorming, Consensus, Dense (a), Kings and Queens, Mission Statement, Opinion, Quagmire, Quantification, Queen Bee, Yappers (2);*

f) the principal faces pressure from the school board and superintendent to be cutting edge, but the knife-blade of innovation dulls quickly and easily; *see Fads (Educational), Flip Flops (2), Innovation, Jurisdiction, Leading Edge, School Board Members;*

see Backbone.

PROFESSIONAL DAYS These non-instructional days provide an opportunity for teachers to hobnob with colleagues and eat lunch in a restaurant with napkins on the table; *see Gossip, Lunch at a Restaurant, Workshops and Seminars, Yogi.*

PROFESSIONAL LEARNING COMMUNITY Using a tautology can generate effective edubabble. Attempted explanations of the characteristics of a professional learning community are excellent examples. Since tautologies express material by simply repeating it in a different way, they contribute to no further understanding. Such gems as, "There was a lot of frozen ice on the road," or "Please prepay in advance," only add unnecessary verbiage. When tautologies are used to explain the meaning of supposedly profound educational activity, the words can sound important until one listens or reads carefully. When asked to define professional learning communities, proponents often resort to meaningless tautologies such as:

a) "a community of professionals working together to learn about teaching";
b) "professionals supporting each other in learning";
c) "learners seeking professional growth in a community atmosphere";
d) "a learning community of professionals."

To add a different tautology to enhance explanation, "The repetitive variations can go on and on"; *see Exemplar, Keener.*

PSYCHOBABBLE Proficiency in this communication technique is a prized skill. A specialist can readily attach impressive-sounding syndromes and disorders to what was once simple student misbehavior. If classroom teachers are searching for answers to help work more effectively with a student, they will not find any answers from a source using and abusing this lingo; *see Counselors, Diphthong, Edubabble, Laws of Bureaucracy (c), Syndrome.*

PSYCHOMOTOR DOMAIN Despite the literal interpretation, this phrase does not refer to a storage place for crazy engines in the mechanics shop.

PUNCTUALITY There is a direct correlation between those teachers who complain the most about student tardiness and those who are regularly late for staff meetings.

Q

QUAGMIRE An apt description for the incredibly slow and tedious staff meeting debates on critical educational issues such as garbage in the hallways, duty rosters, attendance monitoring, coffee fund payment, and the location and format of the next staff party; *see Consensus, Mission Statement, Principal (e).*

QUAINT IDEAS / QUAINT TECHNOLOGY

1. Contemporary teachers may view several educational ideas of the past as nothing more than quaint. Topping the list could be the idea of teachers as role models, on and off the job; and the hidden curriculum, where teacher dress and deportment was believed to have an impact on developing positive student behavior; *see Hidden Curriculum.*
2. If ancient ideas were not strange enough, what about pitiable technology from years past? Who would write questions using an implement that

deposited dusty particles onto a blackboard? Who would use a writing implement that needed to be sharpened by a grinder-like gadget? Who would use a projection unit where the teacher had to erase the writing by hand using a wet cloth? *see Chalk, Overhead Projector, Pencil, Techno-Gadgets.*

QUALIFICATIONS Any person who believes that teacher qualifications do not matter should suffer through one of the following behaviors from non-teacher guest speakers who:

a) drone on in a monotone voice, oblivious to the total disinterest of students;
b) take ten minutes to answer a student question when a simple ten second response would have sufficed;
c) utilize vocabulary at least three years beyond the oldest student in the audience;
d) fire off inappropriate language to appear "cool" to high school students;
e) issue thinly-veiled propaganda to impressionable groups of teenagers in the name of social justice or activism; *see Guest Speaker Negativity;*
f) read to a group of elementary students with a level of excitement matching the home crowd at a football game with their team trailing 49-3 late in the fourth quarter.

QUALITY CIRCLES Proving that business can match the fads found in education, quality circles were the management rage in the latter part of the twentieth century. This was largely propelled by the perceived quality of Japanese products and the success of Japanese businesses. A number of factors led to the demise of the practice in the United States, one of which was less than favorable progress of Japanese companies over the last few decades. This did not deter education researchers, who are almost always late hopping on management fads and frequently revise the terminology to ensure a better fit with education. The push to "empower" teachers was the educational spin-off of the business-oriented quality circle movement. To no surprise the fad met with the same demise as its managerial counterpart; *see Empowerment, Quality Control.*

QUALITY CONTROL Several ultra-conservative thinkers believe schools should utilize a business model to make them more efficient. These include quality control measures regarding teaching competence. Unfortunately educating young people and measuring the result is not as simple as calculating the number of cars sold or money deposited. Given the number of automobile recalls and the financial meltdown of 2008, perhaps the auto and financial industry should analyze their own quality control; *see Accountability, Data-Driven Decision Making, Number Fudgers, Quantification, Standards (Setting of).*

QUANTIFICATION One rule dominates this new trend in determining educational success; if the goal can be measured then it is good. If there is no product, or one that cannot be measured, the goal should not exist since it is clearly not important. If there is logic buried somewhere in these arguments, it is difficult to find; *see Accountability, Benchmarking, Data-Driven Decision Making, Diving Into the Data, Number Crunchers, Principal (e), Standards (Setting of).*

QUEASY No matter how many years of teaching experience have been concluded, there is always a quirky knot in the stomach the night before the first day of school. This may be the result of nervous anticipation or the alcohol consumed over the last weekend of the summer holiday; *see Beer, Wine.*

QUEEN BEE Female by definition and therefore more prevalent in elementary schools, this colleague determines the thoughts and activity of the drones in the school. Though the hive leader is not as powerful as the secretary or janitor, the principal often pays special homage to this opinion leader; *see Consensus, Division (b), Principal (e), Recycling, Yappers (2).*

QUEENSLAND While teachers in northern American states are slogging away with cold playground duty in January and February, teachers in this Australian state are enjoying summer holiday, lolling around on a beach and reading trashy novels. A professional exchange for the two months would be a wonderful mid-year break, though finding a Queensland teacher to agree may prove to be difficult; *see Grisham, Harlequin Romance.*

QUEST FOR EXCELLENCE Though far from a top priority, teachers may have noticed that a school must have a mission statement so the organization, "Knows where it's going." While this may seem self-evident, some people enjoy debating the topic. The quest for excellence, fostering excellence, maximizing excellence, nurturing excellence, the outstanding pursuit of excellence, or similarly garbled edubabble phrases will likely be included. It does not matter if the school succeeds in the quest. Parents and teachers will be told that the adventure is in the journey; *see Edubabble, Mission Statement, Opinion, Outstanding, Yappers (2).*

QUESTIONS (STUDENT) Remember the adage that there are no stupid questions? That was nonsense. There are any number of worthless student questions: those that have nothing to do with the topic at hand, those meant to disrupt the class, those meant to embarrass the teacher or other students, those meant to shock with profanity, those meant to . . . the point should be made. Telling the class there are no stupid questions is . . . well . . . stupid. Forewarned is forearmed; *see Classroom Management, Multi-Tasking.*

QUIET TIME An ideal, resembling a utopia never fulfilled. The closest a teacher will ever come to living the dream is when the class is watching a video or when the "Orator" is in full swing; *see Classroom Management, Noise, Orator.*

QUOTES ON EDUCATION (ANCIENT GREEK PHILOSOPHERS) Rolling eyes upward is the usual teacher response when hearing the word philosophy. Expanding the term to education philosophy will result in a scornful grimace. Adding ancient to the mix will send most teachers scurrying from the room. This is unfortunate since the ancient Greek philosophers may be more relevant to contemporary educational issues than many believe. Teachers may wish that current leaders shared the same level of support for education as three of the most famous ancient Greek philosophers.

1. "The roots of education are bitter, but the fruit is sweet"; (Aristotle).
2. "If a man neglects education he walks lame to the end of his life"; (Plato).
3. "Education is the kindling of a flame, not the filling of a vessel"; (Socrates).

Q-SORT A particularly effective term for those proficient in edubabble, this process supposedly provides a systematic study of participant viewpoints (such as teachers), by sorting the importance of an attribute, project, or behavior in relation to other information. Involving worker participation supposedly promotes democratic decision making. An added benefit is that the entire process sounds technical and managerial; *see Edubabble, Empowerment, Quality Circles.*

R

RAIN DAYS Outside activity at recess at elementary schools may not be feasible due to inclement weather. Forced to be inside during play time, the children's noise and exuberance can create a din in the hallways that rivals those of the teachers in the staffroom; *see Duty, Recess, Yappers (1).*

RANDOM SELECTION Given the theatrics, hyperbole, and maneuvering of a few dominant teachers during class placement meetings at elementary schools, random selection to assign students may be a fairer system. One potential approach could be a neutral third party who selects little balls from transparent containers with student names written on them, similar to those used in bingo halls. At least in bingo only a few people accuse the caller of self-interest or believe the system to be rigged in favor of the loudest or most cunning player in the hall; *see Consensus, Division (b), Queen Bee.*

READING (TEACHING OF) Primary teachers are the true specialists in this pedagogical challenge. When trying to teach reading, most middle school and all high school teachers resemble a track coach providing valuable assistance and insight with statements such as "Run faster." When it comes to teaching reading the high school teacher who exhorts students to "Read louder" is not likely providing much help; *see Track and Field.*

READING (TECHNICAL MANUALS) English teachers are part of a group least likely to be able to decipher technical manuals. Raised on literature, these colleagues can discuss the symbolism in D.H. Lawrence poems, the characterization in Dickens' novels, and the sweeping nature of a Tolstoy epic. Yet they have difficulty understanding the instruction manual for programming a television or assembling a barbecue. Those who write technical manuals seem incapable of dumbing down the writing to the point where it can be understood by the average English teacher. The switch to cartoon-like drawings instead of written language has been slightly more effective in helping the dullards; *see Functional Literacy.*

RECESS This break time is welcomed by all teachers, except those on playground duty; *see Duty, Food Police (1), Java, Mug.*

RECRUITING Effective recruiting requires marketing that tantalizes potential customers about how much better off they would be at one school as opposed to another. Teachers and principals should forget about filling glossy brochures with reams of data on academic achievement and focus on what really counts - the success of sports teams, especially football and basketball. A photo of a smiling female teenager can also add much-needed luster. It is not that photos of Music or Theatrical productions should be totally ignored, but these should comprise no more than one-third the total of sports shots. A photo or two of a Science or Robotics lab is helpful but no one is interested in a picture of a Math or English class; *see Football Team, Marketing.*

RECYCLING The following escapade is an example of a good idea gone bad. After an enthusiastic elementary school staff discussion dominated by ten percent of the teachers, the school "decides" to recycle lunch waste as part of an active environmental awareness program. The principal fires off a few parent notices and the teachers talk to their classes. There is considerable support since only a moron would be opposed to recycling.

The school does not have enough money for proper compost containers but the zealots argue that garbage cans will suffice. The program is enthusiastically supported and students and staff dump their waste into the large containers. Unfortunately, no one has determined what will happen to the waste when the cans are full. Trash collection schedules are difficult to change and pick-up would destroy the entire point of the project which is to keep the food waste out of a landfill.

In the meantime, the food waste begins to smell. This is not very appealing to children or staff. Three children with olfactory issues become ill. One staff member launches a complaint through the union's health and safety committee. Bugs, rodents, feral cats, and stray dogs (not to mention bears in some locales), have differing views than humans about the smelly food waste. To them it is breakfast, lunch, and dinner all rolled into one easy package. Soon the school is inundated with more annoying and predatory varmints than can be managed. Pest control specialists are brought in to eliminate the problem and spray buckets of pesticide and insecticide in the building and on the school grounds. Ten more children and two teachers become ill. A union grievance is launched. Angry parents send a letter to the school board.

At the next staff meeting a new idea for an alternative pro-environment program is proposed to enthusiastic head-bobbing. Rinse and reuse; *see Consensus, Environmental Correctness, Queen Bee, Unforeseen Consequences.*

REFLECTIVE LISTENING There remain those who believe this form of practiced listening enhances communication and understanding. In an attempt to understand the speaker, the listener bounces the idea back, much like a mirror reflecting an image. Alas, one or two workshops on the technique will not make for skillful use. After the speaker keeps hearing numerous variations of the listener stating, "So what I hear you saying is . . ." the logical assumption is that the listener is either dim-witted or hearing impaired; *see Counselors, Fads (Educational).*

REFORM SCHOOL A facility that serviced disruptive and anti-social youth on the road to a life of crime, these schools and the philosophy supporting them are outdated. Now, thanks to more enlightened ideas, these troubled young men and women sit in normal classes in regular schools where they have the opportunity to market their wares or display their specialized talents to a much wider audience; *see Classroom Management, Gum, Nurturing Environment.*

REGULATIONS Not always keen on regulatory hindrances, common teacher reactions are:

a) for those in elementary education, ignore the fire-prevention regulations that permit only a specified percentage of wall space to be covered; *see Fire Drill;*
b) for those in high school, ignore copyright regulations that permit only minor portions of books to be photocopied;
c) for all, ignore distribution warnings on movie DVDs that the copy is for home audiences only.

RELEVANCE This topic of debate amongst curriculum theorists has involved few, if any, classroom teachers. Those stressing auto-relevance seem to have the upper hand, arguing that everything taught must provide instant gratification and immediate relevance to every student. This eliminates much material related to mathematics, philosophy, art history, literature, and composition, and puts the teacher in direct competition for the entertainment dollar with sports, fashion, and movies; *see Art, Curriculum, Grisham, Internet, Math for the Masses, Oprah, Robotics, Safety Education, Television Screen.*

RENEGADES These are the colleagues who ignore the ever-present aura of educational correctness and teach spelling, phonics, and grammar, use drills for teaching mathematics, and insist students re-write essays. Using tactics borrowed from the hit-and-run of guerrilla warfare, these rebels are difficult to apprehend. When caught, they refuse to speak and demand to see their lawyer; *see A (Letter Grade), Educational Correctness, Phonics, Whole Language Approach.*

REPORT CARDS A method of information transfer to parents, reporting has until recently resisted the ease and spread of electronic communication. For elementary teachers, evenings and weekends should be booked well in advance to avoid the feeling that a teacher may have a life away from the job; *see Abacus, Accountability, Hard Copy, Knee-Deep Syndrome.*

ROBOTICS What language would most students select today, Latin or Spanish? What Social Studies option would they choose, Renaissance History or Criminology? If given a Home Economics choice would students pick Sewing or Foods and Nutrition? Hmm, what a dilemma facing the teen of today, forced to choose between Metalwork and Robotics; *see Frills, Latin, Relevance.*

ROBUST Like a great deal of edubabble, this once-popular description came, never conquered, and left with little fanfare. For a short period of time, there was a need for "robust" research, "robust" data, "robust" assessment, and even "robust" coffee. The speed at which the descriptor passed from the lexicon was . . . well . . . "robust"; *see Edubabble.*

RULE BREAKERS

1. Revered by most of their adolescent peers, there are few detection systems these students cannot beat. Ruthless and cunning, the risk takers have little respect for the rules, making them viable candidates to be future CEO's or CFO's of major corporations; *see Frankenstein, Informal Leader, Number Fudgers, Self-Esteem (Student).*
2. These students did not have as much fun at elementary school as one may think. It is difficult for a child to break a rule without a mouthy peer tattling. The squealers will then berate the teacher with a memorized litany of all the school rules, some of which the adult had either forgotten or didn't know in the first place; *see Budging in Line, Tattlers and Squealers.*

RULERS These instruments have far greater utility than simply helping students draw straight lines. Children with oral fixations can stick them in their mouths and hungry ones can sink their teeth into them. They can also be used as swords, clubs, or catapults to launch objects across the room; *see Halo, UFO (1).*

RURAL SCHOOLS (ONE ROOM) A few of these extremely small schools still exist and working in one has several benefits, including being both the principal and teacher. If this unique employment relationship does not result in mercifully brief staff meeting debates, seek immediate medical advice; *see Consensus, Mission Statement, Quagmire, Yappers (1).*

S

SAFETY EDUCATION A prime example of relevance for contemporary curriculum theorists, this program emphasizes fire drills, street crossing, and bicycle safety in elementary schools, easily within the teacher's comfort zone. It is the lessons on private body parts and "personal relationships" which can provide anxiety, especially when the fifth or sixth grade child is asking questions that never entered the teacher's mind until university years, if then. Sexually oriented topics that reach far beyond the old-fashioned biological body-part talk may max out the knowledge base of some teachers and the comfort zone of many others. Not even psychobabble works on these pre-pubescent students who are far too worldly to be taken in by such nonsense.

In high schools the curriculum shifts to drinking and driving prevention, date rape, condom use, and proper procedures for disarming attackers in school and the mall. The lessons become really complex when entering the realm of gender fluidity and genitalia alteration.

This is one of the few areas where specialist assistance can actually help, though proper personnel selection is paramount. Good luck finding someone who is not so boring to lull the students to sleep, and not so controversial to cause a placard-waving parent parade calling for a teacher's head on a platter; *see Gum, I Don't Know (Poor Responses-a), Nurturing Environment, Relevance.*

SCHOOL BOARD MEMBERS Occasionally effective, sometimes well-meaning, and often media savvy, these people may be looking for a leap into civic politics. Usually running unopposed or elected by appalling levels of voter turnout, they can boss the superintendent about and jab their fingers into all kinds of educational pies. The perceived authority can act as a narcotic for many and more than a few can get drunk on real or imagined power. If teachers know these people and see them in school (an unlikely combination), they should smile nicely, make innocuous comments about how wonderful the students are and find a way of exiting the conversation. You never know the unfortunate result of what the teacher thought to have been an innocent comment; *see Government Interference, Jurisdiction, Parent Council (c), Politicians, Unforeseen Consequences, Wits on Education.*

SECRETARY *see Names and Titles, Office Workers.*

SELF-ESTEEM (STUDENT) The emphasis on this attribute is a classic case of the triumph of means over ends. If you build a student's self-esteem, no matter how unjustified, it is good action on the part of the teacher and positive for the student. Unfortunately, there seems to be no lack of people with high levels of self-esteem who do very little good for society. These include mafia bosses, corporate lawyers, rap icons, and narcissistic movie stars; *see Number Fudgers, Rule Breakers (1).*

SELF-ESTEEM (TEACHER) If a teacher waits for praise from a school board official he or she will be waiting a long time. Those hungry for positive recognition in the media will remain empty-bellied. Those yearning for a politician to deliver on education promises will spend a career pining. Keep self-esteem intact by knowing good work is accomplished every day. The few times that students, colleagues, or the principal extend kudos will be akin to a shot of adrenaline in the arm that will keep a teacher energized for a surprising length of time; *see Altruism, Boss, Fault Police, Journalists, Teachers' High, Undaunted, Utility Infielder.*

SEVENTH-GRADE GIRLS At one time these students might have been interested in schoolwork; but not now. Suddenly, previously ignored body parts, both their own and those of others, appear to have changed. Boys look different; *really* different. Even Mr. Brody, the young Math teacher seems to have changed and that is too weird to even talk about. Body hair grows where there was none before. The brain keeps telling the eyes to note every nuance of speech and behavior in others so as to better detect hidden meaning. A previously smooth chest displays bulges. There is a sudden urge to buy shoes and purses.

Good luck to the teacher trying to teach this tortured human being; *see Dramatic Performance (b), Eighth-Grade Boys, Hormones With Feet, Middle School, No Man's Land, Notes in Class, Pension Knowledge.*

SHOP TALK This overused conversation amongst teachers is especially evident at Saturday night parties attended by interesting people from all walks of life. Huddled in a corner, the teachers discuss educational issues that would have a non-teacher bored in less than thirty seconds; *see Altruism, Gossip, Kindred Spirit, Veteran Teachers (a), Zealot.*

SHOW AND TELL / SHARING TIME A useful time-muncher at the primary level, this activity can range from enlightening to incredibly boring. This technique should be avoided when teaching high school students, unless the teacher is brave, foolish, or has tenure.

SICK DAYS The number of occasions that these days are abused does not equal the number of days teachers arrive at work when they should be at home. The reason may be linked to old fashioned work ethic or be the result of more practical concerns. It is often more time consuming to plan for a replacement than to arrive at work and struggle through the day. There may also be a bizarre desire for a little payback; reversing the usual behavioral pattern by sneezing and coughing over the students; *see Germ Factory, Occupational Hazards (b), Sneeze, Vacation (2).*

SNEEZE Primary age students may not be proficient at schoolwork but they are very adept at spreading germs, usually in close proximity to their teacher; *see Germ Factory, Occupational Hazards (b), Sick Days, Vacation (2).*

SNOW DAYS It seems a bit excessive to hope for a hurricane, tornado, or earthquake in order to be rewarded with a day off school. But a relatively common but heavy snowfall in certain climes can mean a precious day at home prompted by inconvenience rather than horrific disaster. After completing shoveling tasks, a teacher can settle in a quiet abode, sipping hot chocolate, watching day-time TV, and reading a trashy novel, all the while hoping for more of the white stuff to hit the ground; *see Grisham, Harlequin Romance, Television.*

SOCIETAL EXPECTATIONS The public wants the very best school system; they just don't want to pay for it. The politicians want the same thing; a Cadillac system at economy car prices. Amazingly, the system almost delivers; *see Budget, Politicians, Teacher, Volunteer Labor, Zeitgeist.*

SONGS ABOUT TEACHERS While there are a plethora of movies featuring teachers, and even a few ancient TV shows, there are virtually no well-known songs about the profession or those who work in it. There is opportunity for the musically inclined educator to seize the day and compose what could become the "anthem" of the teaching brigade. The first major decision would be the style chosen. The possibilities are vaudevillian, hip-hop, twangy country, rap, heavy metal, or schlocky musical-theater pop. Another possibility is to rework the lyrics of well-known songs. *You Can't Always Get What You Want,* by the Rolling Stones could highlight budget cuts. Pink Floyd's memorable lyrics associated with "We don't need no education," could be reworked to describe teachers being force-fed workshops given by non-teacher "experts." Leonard Cohen's *Hallelujah* would be a fine song for the final day of the school year; *see Movies About Teachers, Old TV Shows About Teachers, Workshops and Seminars.*

SPECIALLY TRAINED SPECIAL EDUCATION TEACHERS There are several many education teachers with highly specialized training. They are housed in a special education wing of a special school district building and provide specialized services to special children. The classroom teacher in a regular school does not realize these colleagues exist nor would they understand, or even be able to spell, the services rendered.

SPUTNIK In 1957, at the height of the cold war, the Soviet Union launched the first satellite into space. Shocked and shaken, the American public clamored to catch up to the "evil" communists in science and technology. Bucketloads of money flowed to schools for science education. Perhaps this generosity can be repeated. If the Russians once again provide a threat to western global hegemony, schools may benefit. Could Mr. Putin be a key figure in providing support, no matter how unintended, for American public schools? *see Societal Expectations.*

STANDARD DEVIATION It does not matter that most teachers never understood this statistical measurement when it was taught in university. Not surprisingly, given the high level of importance placed on it in teacher preparation programs, it has no practical value in the day-to-day job. Occasionally the phrase can be a handy "term-dropper" when engaging in edubabble; *see Edubabble, Median, Zero (c).*

STANDARDS (SETTING OF) This process makes for great politics and interesting media coverage as everyone grapples with how the mythical average student should perform at a particular point in time. There is more debate about standards and performance of children and youth than those of adults who are also funded by the taxpayer. What should the average soldier, postal worker, civil servant, police officer, or professor be able to do at a given point in time in their career? *see Government Interference, Quality Control, Quantification.*

SYNDROME Since this term only describes behavior, a teacher can be sure that several students in the class are afflicted with one syndrome or another. Those proficient in psychobabble revel in phrases to describe behavior such as, "Anti-Authority Syndrome" or "Cry and Whine Syndrome" or "Bathroom Averse Syndrome." While the need to discuss such behavior provides highly paid specialists with employment, the pyschobabble of an hour-long meeting does nothing to help a classroom teacher work effectively with the specific student. In a sense, the classroom teacher suffers from "Abandonment Syndrome"; *see Attention Deficit Disorder, Counselors, Edubabble, Psychobabble.*

T

TATTLERS AND SQUEALERS When a teacher is on playground duty, is it critically important to know that sixth-grader Brian is playing with friends in the primary area, or that Susan kicked a soccer ball into the forest? In class, is it critical that the teacher is aware that a boy was drawing stick men when it was reading time, or a girl was coloring the sun green when it was supposed to be yellow? The teacher may not think so, but the tattler/squealer does. Not only are these students eager to throw their peers under the bus, they await the anticipated punishment with great expectation, often displaying disappointment when the sanction is not nearly as severe as anticipated. One wonders what becomes of these children in their later lives; *see Aides (b), Budging in Line, Duty, Rule Breakers (2).*

TEACHER This complex position requires the skills of a social worker, police officer, counselor, referee, warden, mother, father, professor, nurse, psychologist, recreation director, and baby-sitter. When not performing these tasks, the teacher is free to teach; *see Altruism, Blame Industry, Fault, Judge and Jury, Multi-Tasking, Societal Expectations, Umpire (Professional Baseball), Undaunted, Volunteer Labor. Zealot.*

TEACHERS' HIGH Caffeine is a widely utilized source to produce a mild buzz. While wine and beer can help dull the pain, they can cause more the following morning. For teachers, nothing produces the high that results from attempting numerous ways to assist a child in understanding a difficult concept, and finally succeeding. The smile on the child's face and the sparkle in the eyes when he or she finally states, "I get it now," produces a stream of euphoria-producing endorphins that only a teacher can understand. As with any junkie, the teacher will continue to search diligently for the next fix; *see Altruism, Java, Self-Esteem (Teacher), Undaunted, Valium.*

TECHNO-GADGETS These are indispensable and omnipresent and it is a wonder that teachers could teach and students could learn before these devices were invented. But seamless flow of information does not equate to wisdom and knowledge, and many gadgets serve more as peacock-pluming fashion accoutrements rather than educational tools; *see Abacus, Apple Inc., Fidget, Overhead Projectors, Pencil, Quaint Ideas/Quaint Technology (2), Texting.*

TECHNO-GEEKS This tiny minority of teachers actually like e-learning and all things technical. They can often be seen huddled in the computer lab speaking a language that has only passing similarity to English. These teachers were likely members of the Audio-Visual Club when they were in high school; *see Clubs, Computer-Assisted Instruction, K, Learning Suite.*

TEETH It is common to see gap-toothed primary children eagerly showing their teacher a tooth that has just dropped out of his or her mouth. It is not common, and certainly less pleasant, to see gap-toothed high school students; the missing fang a result of a sports injury or a disagreement-turned dust-up at a weekend bash. It is better not to ask what happened since the reply may be, "You should see the other guy"; *see Football Team.*

TELEVISION Given the long-time position of reverence in the family home, this appliance continues to be a serious competitor to teachers. Unlike public education, the television industry has substantial resources, enabling it to produce an endless supply of drivel with little concern for quality or impact. It also seems immune to critics who desire a semblance of accountability. Given this, television remains a formidable adversary; *see Accountability, Oprah, Oxymorons, Relevance, Snow Days, Television Screen, Ukulele, Wits on Education.*

TELEVISION SCREEN Since students are glued to screens at home, in the van, and at the local arcade, they may regard their teacher as a quirk of nature; resembling an oddly-shaped mobile monitor, or a robotic prototype that walked off the screen of their video-game world; *see Classroom Management, Oprah, Quiet Time, Relevance, Robotics.*

TESTING (STANDARDIZED) When the student results of such tests are high, the politicians take the credit; when they are low, the teachers take the blame; *see Blame Industry, Experts, Politicians, Self-Esteem (Teacher), Societal Expectations.*

TESTOSTERONE POISONING This is a common affliction that hits male students at around thirteen years of age. Many females claim that the poison never leaves a man's body until maturity. This occurs somewhere between ninety and ninety-five years of age; *see Eighth-Grade Boys, Football Team, Jokes, Kayaks and Canoes.*

TESTS (NEW TEACHER) When a teacher has been assigned to a new school it is important that the person plan and prepare for the inevitable teacher tests. First impressions are important and lasting and a willingness to empty the dishwasher and brew pots of coffee are good starts, though more hurdles will come. Did the new teacher remember to bring the "goodies" for the staff meeting? Can he or she use the photocopier without breaking it? Did he or she remember to contribute to the staff social and coffee fund? Failing these tests will make a new teacher's future uncertain and the person may have the unfortunate experience of being "volunteered" to organize the collection of various funds the following year; *see Coffee Fund, First-Year Teacher, Xerox.*

TEXTBOOK There are usually not enough books for every student. These resources are often lost, misplaced, damaged, destroyed, or otherwise rendered useless by students, and at times, colleagues.

TEXTBOOK (TEACHER'S COPY) An extremely valued commodity, the special book gives answers to questions a teacher might not be able to work out independently. Students value these copies for the same reason so the books are best kept under lock and key; *see Atlas, Filing Cabinet, Intelligence Level, Keys.*

TEXTING Lesson plans may soon need to include breaks for middle and high school students to allow them to text about really important material. This includes thumb-tapping about what was consumed for breakfast, who in the class is wearing the coolest jeans, and the location of the weekend party; *see Classroom Management, Lesson Plans, Notes in Class, Techno-Gadgets, Time Out.*

TIME OUT When students are misbehaving they are occasionally placed in a form of solitary confinement to contemplate their misdeeds in unconnected silence. With a cell phone buried in a pocket, the student has a world of information before him or her and there is a distinct possibility of learning more in solitary than sitting in a crowded classroom; *see Internet, Relevance, Techno-Gadgets, Texting.*

TRACK AND FIELD Teachers should not be alarmed at the potential carnage caused by errant shot puts to student heads and javelins to chests. Track and field has many positive attributes. The teacher gets to take the class outside when it is usually warm and sunny. There is opportunity to display teacher knowledge by barking out meaningless support phrases such as, "Run faster," or, "Throw it farther next time." If you are not trained in Physical Education no one expects you to use the dangerous equipment. Best of all, after running around in the sun, the students are usually quiet and serene when they return inside; *see Quiet Time, Reading (Teaching of).*

TROPHY CASE (SPORTS) It can take schools a bit of time to adjust to new trends, in this case, about forty to fifty years. Perhaps there might be a more meaningful way to recognize athletic excellence than dishing out virtually identical athletic trophies as those dating back to the early-mid 1900's.

There are few, if any high schools that do not have at least one trophy case, and in many there can be as many as six or more. There are fewer than six students who will ever look in one. Every year the display case is opened (presuming a coach can find the key), and the trophy is dusted off to be given to a beaming student at an awards ceremony. Photos are taken, the trophy is engraved with the winner's name (most of the time), before being returned to the case to gather dust until the next year, ignored by staff and students; *see Latin.*

TWENTY-FIRST CENTURY LEARNING This new educational buzz phrase is a prime example of the meaningless self-congratulatory sloganeering of edubabble. After all, boasting about providing twentieth-century learning in the twenty-first century would sound silly at best. In the second decade of this century auto manufacturers hardly boast about producing twentieth-century cars. Communication enterprises do not brag about being more efficient than the telegraph. It should not be much of a stretch to assume that the education system is promoting learning for the century in which it was operating; *see Edubabble, Under Construction/School of the Future.*

U

UBER PLANNING There are a few high school teachers who are so well planned that they know in September the textbook page the class will be working on in February. This is despite the inevitability that some classes are populated by quick-learning students, while those in other classes of the same subject will learn at a slower pace and require more time to reach proficiency. This variance in student ability is of little consequence to the uber-planner; the content is the content. The flexibility of this tiny minority of teachers closely resembles that of an iron bar; *see Mean (2).*

UFO

1. Unidentified Flying Object: on occasion these will zip about the classroom accompanied by student giggles. The origins of such phenomena will, despite the teacher's best efforts, often

remain unknown; *see Halo, Jason, Judge and Jury, Pareto Principle.*

2. Unidentified Foreign Object: these are usually found in the back cavity of student desks or in the bottom of lockers. Origins are most likely components of a half-eaten lunch which carbon dating would reveal to be at least five months old. Teachers should use plastic gloves to remove the material or plead for janitorial support; *see Carpeting, Fruit Flies, Janitor, Oranges.*

UKULELE This is a favorite instrument for beginner music programs since, unlike recorders, there is usually very little saliva or other body fluids involved. The ukulele's similarity to the guitar also has appeal for those students realistically contemplating a career as a rock star. They will do their best to use the instrument to mimic their chord-thumping music hero; *see Elementary Concerts, Frills,*

ULTIMATUM Issuing ultimatums is rarely a good idea. After barking a phrase such as, "The next person who makes a sound is going to get a detention," the offending student will inevitably be the quietest, most meek child in the class who utters an "Oops" when dropping a crayon on the floor. Stuck with following through on the threat, the teacher will appear unfair, intolerant, and mean-spirited, all of which are accurate descriptors; *see Classroom Management, Mean (2), Noise, Notes in Class, Uber-Planner.*

UMPIRE (PROFESSIONAL BASEBALL) This job has eerie similarities to teaching. Requiring good judgment, quick decisions, and a loud voice to control others, the umpire has to deal with many people who can best be described as difficult and some who are nothing but spoiled brats. The high levels of verbal abuse hurled at the umpire adds to the occupational similarities; *see Blame Industry, Fault, Politicians, Teacher, Testing (Standardized).*

UNDAUNTED This is an apt description of most teachers and high-functioning aides. Despite few supplies, outdated books, faulty equipment, parentless students, and meddling reformers, they plow on through the fields of students, hoping to plant a seed or two of skill, knowledge, or inspiration; *see Aides (a), Altruism, Self-Esteem (Teacher), Teachers' High, Teacher.*

UNDER CONSTRUCTION / SCHOOL OF THE FUTURE School district officials regularly trot out their visioning acumen when a new school is being built. This phraseology is another example of the meaningless drivel and sloganeering of edubabble. What government in their right mind would provide taxpayer funding to construct a new school of the past? *see Design, Edubabble.*

UNFORESEEN CONSEQUENCES House renovations almost always result in increased costs when compared to what was originally planned. Ripping out a wall may require further alterations or reveal damage not foreseen. Similarly, there are multitudes of examples of unforeseen consequences as a result of educational change. Were adequate resources in place for the new course or program? Was training provided for teachers? Was the resultant impact on facilities, equipment, and budgets taken into account? Given that non-educators often make the critical decisions about educational change without input from teachers, the frequent answer to these and other questions is often, "No"; *see Education Professors, Innovation, Nadir, Politicians, Recycling, School Board Members.*

UNIFORMITY OF THOUGHT Teachers marry fellow teachers. Friends of teachers are teachers. Children of teachers often become teachers. Attitudes are shared, opinions supported, and political views synchronized. The result is a belief system resembling a hard-shelled cocoon where external opinions and contrary views are as spurned as they are unwelcome; *see Altruism, Conservative-Thinking Liberals, Teacher, Undaunted, University (1).*

UNION / ASSOCIATION An association of colleagues legally entitled to take portions of paychecks. In return the teacher has the opportunity to attend stimulating, high-interest meetings where rational debate and informed discussion are supposedly utilized; *see Brainstorming, Jurisdiction, Oligarchy (Law of), Politicos.*

UNIVERSITY

1. The place of higher learning where education students conduct a search for a future spouse. The romantic link is often initiated in the university pub followed by dorm action, not from any intellectual connection forged in the library; *see Uniformity of Thought.*
2. The campus where teacher memories of student days focus on social life with little or nothing retained from coursework. As a teacher, these ex-pupils complain about their current students focusing more on their social life and not enough on coursework; *see Internet, Encyclopedia Online (2).*
3. An educational institution whose leaders seem far more interested in linking with wealthy donors and acquiring research grants than with competent teaching.

UNKEMPT This term can be used to describe an increasing number of students. It may be a sign of poverty or neglect, or in older students, one of self-expression. When working with young children, beginning teachers should follow the lead of many veteran colleagues and keep snacks in the desk drawer. These children may need them.

UNTRUTHFUL STATEMENTS A teacher is well advised against telling a parent that their child is lying. There is a spark to the word that ignites parent acrimony.

An angry retort, accompanied by an aggressive posture and threatening timbre will likely be, "Are you calling my child a *liar?*" This is stated as if the teacher had accused the parent, not the child. A far more appropriate opening statement would be, "I believe (insert name – do not use the possessive 'your child'), has told an untruthful statement." A milder response from the parent is likely. Euphemisms are clearly effective which helps explain their long and storied history in activities far removed from education. There have been many military routs described as "strategic withdrawals," narcotics smugglers who describe their business as "import-export," or stolen goods that "fell off the back of a truck"; *see Excuses, Halo, Jason, Judge and Jury.*

UPHOLSTERY *see Vinyl Upholstery.*

URINAL Some male primary students lack experience using these receptacles and their aim may be off the mark or miss entirely. If there is only one male staff member and no day-time janitor, extra unpaid work may be required; *see Health and Safety, Janitor.*

UTILITY INFIELDER Never a starter at one position, yet able to slip into a variety of roles, this person is a valuable member of any baseball team. The equivalent position in education, the substitute teacher, is less likely to feel part of the school team, less likely to feel valued, and less likely to be noticed by colleagues unless he or she commits countless errors; *see Self-Esteem (Teacher).*

V

VACATION This is a time when travel costs such as airline tickets and hotel rooms rise. Before the fun can begin, a period of adjustment is necessary to catch up on the illness a teacher did not have time for during the school year; *see Altruism, Germ Factory, Occupational Hazards (b), Sick Days, Sneeze.*

VALENTINE'S DAY Paradoxically this special day of romance is especially exciting for primary age children who, while years away from puberty, enjoy making cards and drawing hearts. Teachers should avoid handing out stickers of cupid. The chubby cherub may not meet today's culinary, political, or educational correctness standards: after all, he is overweight and most often naked. Additionally, the arrow he holds could be construed as a weapon; *see Educational Correctness.*

VALIUM Surprisingly this depressant is not the drug of choice for the vast majority of teachers, falling far behind the readily available stimulant, caffeine; *see Coffee Machine, Java, Mug, Teachers' High, Veteran Teachers (d).*

VAN GOGH This artist has much appeal today. Unlike the work of Picasso, the students can usually discern what Van Gogh was attempting to paint, though they may believe the image to be a grainy, poorly done digital remake. Furthermore, angst-riddled teenagers can relate to any weird, cool guy who cuts his ear off and whose friends hung around on tropical beaches creating works that are worth millions of dollars. This guy is cool with a capital C; *see Art, Relevance.*

VARNISHING ROOM Woodwork teachers should check this room at least once a class period to snare any students who turn off the fans, being more intent on taking in the fumes than varnishing their project. It may also be a good idea to occasionally check the room after school for any teachers in need of a little mind-alteration after a long day in the classroom. Give colleagues a warning before considering reporting the transgression to the Health and Safety Committee. If the principal is found sucking in the scent, bargaining (blackmailing), for new equipment may be a good idea; *see Health and Safety, Java, Whiteboards.*

VERSACE, GUCCI, AND ARMANI Sounding more like an Italian law firm than a trio of famous designers, teachers never wear their fashion creations, principally for two reasons:

a) teachers do not have fat wallets. The price point for the clothing and accessories is far beyond their means and available only to people working in positions of great benefit to society such as baseball players, tax-evasion lawyers, and hedge fund managers; *see Informal Leader, Pay Slip (2), Self-Esteem (Student);*

b) for many teachers, high fashion appeals to those who are weak-minded and easily led, and teachers tend to favor the practical over the sexy. Many male teachers believe that wearing a tweed jacket, corduroy pants, and cheap brogues is still a fashion statement (it is though not in the way they think). When hitting the nightlife, female teachers usually wear a dress or skirt more likely purchased at Sears than Nordstrom; *see Conservative-Thinking Liberals, Dress, Fads (Fashion), Goth Look, Jeans, Jocks and Jockettes;*

see Goth Look.

VETERAN TEACHERS These colleagues can be identified by the following characteristics:

a) they do not talk about work during staff socials; *see Shop Talk;*

b) they have the most comfortable chairs in the staff room; *see Vinyl-Upholstery, Wise Sage;*

c) they always have the DVD machine signed out on the Friday afternoon before a holiday; *see DVDs;*

d) they never brew a pot of coffee; *see Coffee Machine, Java, Tests (New Teacher), Valium;*

e) they can rattle off the remaining work time before retirement; *see Dramatic Performance (d), Pension Knowledge.*

VICE-PRINCIPAL The workhorse job in the school, the vice-principal does much behind the scenes to make the principal look good. What is noticed by teachers is only the tip of the iceberg; meting out student discipline, completing textbook and equipment inventories, and acting as a hallway monitor. The vice-principal reports directly to the janitor while the principal reports to the secretary; *see Janitor, Meds, Office Reception Area (d), Pareto Principle.*

VINYL LUNCH BAGS Bringing a lunch to school in a paper bag is likely to draw disapproving stares from ecologically sensitive colleagues. These coworkers prefer to bring plastic containers holding salads, store-bought yogurt cylinders, and tetra pack juice boxes in more environmentally correct lunch bags. These sacks have vinyl exteriors, foam insulation, and plastic coating covering the interior; *see Environmental Correctness, Guest Speaker Negativity, Food Police (1).*

VINYL UPHOLSTERY Cloth upholstery sucks in dust, dirt, grime, and lice. Leather-clad furniture is too expensive. Easy to clean, grime resistant, and most importantly, inexpensive, vinyl covering is the material of choice for staffroom furniture. Mismatched style and color is common as the chairs were purchased at different times by various principals with tastes ranging from marginal to truly awful. Chairs with ripped or torn vinyl covering are never thrown out and occupy a corner where they provide a horizontal surface that is used as a convenient dumping ground for the dross of the teacher workplace; *see Veteran Teachers (b).*

VISIONARY A person described by this term frequently trumpets futuristic thinking and innovation. Given the abysmal track record of most educational change, it is remarkable that teachers listen to these people who spend far more time researching, writing, and speaking at conferences than they do teaching; *see Innovation, Leading Edge, Open Area Classrooms/Open Concept School, Unforeseen Consequences, Workshops and Seminars.*

VOLUNTEER LABOR Coaching teams, directing theatrical productions, conducting musical performances, and sponsoring student clubs are volunteer activities in the vast majority of North American schools. Tabulating the sheer volume of hours of free labor would result in a staggering total, a fact rarely considered by students, parents, and politicians; *see Basketball, Clubs, Dance (1), Full Moon Theorist, Golf Team, Government Funding, Musical Theater Royalties, Societal Expectations.*

VOTING FOR STUDENT COUNCIL Though little more than a popularity contest, these elections mirror their adult counterparts in hyperbole, promises made and forgotten, and frequent lackluster performance once the victor is in office. Usually supervised by the sponsor teacher, student council elections are far less likely to be rigged than voting procedures in the vast majority of countries around the world; *see Volunteer Labor.*

VOUCHER SYSTEM Educational reformers of the political far right persuasion dream of implementing this innovation. At the core, this system will provide a voucher to parents who can shop for the school best suited to their needs, just as they do for shoes and tires. This will, of course, provide a range of education "stores", from the school equivalent of Saks to Macys, to Wal Mart. The Orwellian phrase, slightly adjusted, "All students would be equal but some would be more equal than others," will become even more of a stark reality than it is currently; *see Data-Driven Decision Making, Education (Public), Leading Edge, Politicians, Quality Control, Visionary.*

W

WALKING TO SCHOOL Why would any elementary student engage in this activity when a parent can drive them, despite their domicile being only a block or two away from the school? This causes the school parking lot to be a jumbled mess of vehicles at the beginning and end of the day. The only solution appears to be expanding the parking lot and covering the remaining bits of the school field with asphalt. In the words of Joni Mitchell and later the Counting Crows, "You pave paradise, and put up a parking lot."

WALL DISPLAYS To provide an atmosphere conducive to learning, elementary teachers plaster every inch of their classroom walls with student work, posters, charts, diagrams, and photos. This breaks every fire code regulation in existence. The usually rule-conscious elementary teacher does not seem to care. High school teachers put up three posters in September and leave them for the entire year, believing this to be a sufficient attempt at creating a stimulating learning environment; *see Fire Drill, Regulations (a).*

WALL MAPS Pulling this finicky learning resource down is a simple task. Getting the stubborn display to remain in position requires considerable skill, patience, and practice. Once down, these fickle items often refuse to roll back up, thus reducing the available whiteboard space by at least fifty percent.

WATERING HOLE This is a popular gathering spot on Friday afternoons where teachers can unwind with a few pints of beer or glasses of wine. The *bonhomie* is readily apparent as the group gossip about colleagues who are not present and yak about students. As the alcohol flows and fewer members remain, favorite topics can include the incompetence of the principal, superintendent, or both; *see Beer, Educational Correctness, Gossip, Grapevine, Kids, Neuron Forest, Shop Talk, Whine, Wine.*

WAX Spread on linoleum hallways during breaks in the school year, this substance makes the floor shine for the first hour of school re-opening; *see Linoleum.*

WEAPONS (EXTRA-CURRICULAR ACTIVITIES) It is difficult to keep an eager gun-lover down. Despite the controversy surrounding weapons in schools, there remain numerous rifle teams and clubs in American schools. According to their websites, these health-promoting club activities are gaining popularity. In response to a few "Negative-Nellie" parent protesters, the school can always note that guns used in student activities are simply a necessary piece of equipment, just like a baseball glove, volleyball net, or basketball; *see Gum, Kitchen Knives, Nurturing Environment, Valentine's Day.*

WHINE A social lubricant of sorts, this is a shared trait amongst a minority of teachers, often thought to be more numerous due to the quantity of verbiage emanating from so few mouths. It is not to be confused with wine, though there can be a cause and effect between the two; *see Attendance and Punctuality, Opinion, Watering Hole, Wine, Yappers (1).*

WHITEBOARDS The shift from chalk and blackboards to felt markers and whiteboards has eliminated much powder and dust. The change had less to do with employee health than the well-being of computers, which are not as tough or resilient as teachers. The smell from the markers can provide a nice jolt after a long day in the classroom; *see Blackboards, Chalk, Non-Carbon Paper, Varnishing Room.*

WHITE-OUT This material has disappeared from student supply lists. No longer can students get the quick high from the smell or provide a skill test for janitors to rid desks and lockers of the tough substance; *see Janitor, Overhead Projector, Pencil.*

WHOLE LANGUAGE APPROACH This is another fine example of edubabble. One wonders what the alternative is . . . partial language approach? *see Edubabble, Phonics, Renegades.*

WINDOWS Some of the varieties of windows a teacher may encounter are the following:

a) those that allow cold drafts to seep, unimpeded, into the room, (circa 1940's);
b) those designed to open but fail to do so due to the fifteen layers of paint keeping them shut, (circa 1950's); *see Design (2);*
c) those never designed to open to save energy, (circa 1970's);
d) those gargantuan windows that cause a teacher to wear sunglasses on a bright day, (circa 1990's); *see Design (3).*

WINE This is the beverage of choice as a social lubricant at staff parties. Leave the herbal tea (too dull), the beer (too student), and the distilled liquor (too hard core), at home. Spend more than $10.00 on the bottle to avoid appearing too cheap but stay under $20.00 unless an extravagant or snooty reputation is sought; *see Beer, Gossip, Investment Club, Lunch at a Restaurant, Marking (a), Neuron Forest, Teachers' High, Watering Hole, Xmas Staff Parties.*

WISE SAGE Serenity increases noticeably as the retirement date for this veteran teacher approaches. This colleague is well respected and revered, though not necessarily for teaching competence; *see Dress, Veteran Teachers (b).*

WITS ON EDUCATION Teachers will be pleased to know that they have had supporters amongst many famous wits who praise the cause and/or lambaste the decision makers. An example of both is Mark Twain who commented that, "It is noble to teach oneself, but still nobler to teach others," and, "In the first place God made idiots. This was for practice. Then He made school boards."

Other notable American wits who sang teacher's praises are Groucho Marx who said, "I find television very educational. The minute somebody turns it on I go to the library and read a good book." Benjamin Franklin advised, "Learn of the skillful; he that teaches himself has a fool for a master"; *see Home Schooling, Oprah, School Board Members, Television.*

WOMEN IN ADMINISTRATION Women wishing to "rise" in the hierarchy keep smacking their heads on a ceiling, but in each subsequent generation the injury suffered is diminishing:

a) two generations ago, the ceiling blocking "advancement" into administration was made of wood. There was no attempt to pretend it was not there. A woman needed a hard head and a considerable level of tenacity to keep bashing her skull against the hardwood. In the end, what she usually got was a concussion;

b) a generation ago, the ceiling became thin air in the elementary school system as women streamed into administrative roles. It was not quite the same for high school and central office positions. The ceiling was glass, hard to penetrate and difficult to see. A woman desiring a high-school administrative position had to keep thumping her head against the glass, which is a damn hard substance. In the end, what she usually got was a hell of a migraine;

c) now the ceiling for high school and central office leadership positions is made of thin, clear plastic. It is still there, but not nearly as hard as it once was. With luck and persistence, a woman can break through the plastic. In the end, what she will usually get is a bump on the noggin and a headache that can be alleviated with a few Tylenol tablets. A little heat put on the plastic ceiling in the next decade may burn the last vestiges of the material away.

WORK HABITS Teachers, parents and students do not pay nearly enough attention to assessing this attribute. A student receiving a high mark on work habits while receiving a low grade on achievement says a great deal about the individual. Continuing to work diligently while lacking proficiency is a sign of admirable dedication and character, attributes coveted by employers.

When in adult employment, often the A level students are employed by those who consistently achieved at the C level (the B level students work for the government). This makes for interesting discussions regarding comparative affluence at the twenty-year high school reunion; *see Instant Gratification.*

WORKPLACE POISONING This phrase does not refer to putting strychnine in the staffroom coffee. Much more serious, the accused (read guilty), person has allegedly poisoned the workplace through inappropriate comments or behavior. When a teacher is accused, the endless meetings with union leaders, lawyers, and bureaucrats will make the individual seriously consider taking strychnine as a more pleasant and certainly quicker demise; *see Educational Correctness, Jokes.*

WORKSHOPS AND SEMINARS Time may be granted to listen to explanations of the latest innovation or leading-edge idea that is to be crammed down a teacher's throat. A quiet respectful silence is to be observed, no matter how impractical or insane the idea. A teacher can always provide the appropriate response later by ignoring the advice and forgetting about it ten minutes after leaving the parking lot; *see Innovation, Leading Edge, Songs About Teachers, Visionary, Yogi, Zig-Zag (b).*

X

X-BOX It is almost impossible for teachers to compete for student attention against the mayhem and carnage of these "games." Older elementary school children can be found "blowing away" their adversaries and mimicking the extraordinarily realistic violence while "playing" during recess and lunch. Every teacher claims this type of aggressive activity increases when he or she is on duty; *see Duty, Kung Fu, Playground Spats, Recess.*

XEROX Developing a positive relationship with the important and often fickle photocopy machine is critical to teaching success. When upset, the snarling beast makes unnerving noise and displays red inflamed lights. When happy, the creature hums and purrs. Feeding it regularly (it prefers toner to sandwiches), stroking it gently and speaking to it in soft whispers are often successful strategies; *see Tests (New Teacher).*

XMAS In an era of educational and political correctness, teachers may find the school moving away from Christmas concerts to more secular productions. Some innovative approaches to appease those of varying faiths may include school-wide spirituality weeks in which any religion, no matter how obscure; or any cult, no matter how crazy, gets equal time; *see Educational Correctness.*

XMAS STAFF PARTIES It may be tempting to drink copious quantities of cheap wine at the staff party but such behavior is not normally a good idea. A teacher may wind up snuggling with the married politico or enthralling those present with impressive but politically incorrect oratory from the top of a kitchen table. Loudly denouncing the idiocy of the principal when the boss is standing behind, three steps away, is another unfortunate possibility; *see Beer, GPA, Jokes, Neuron Forest, Wine.*

X-TREME SPORTS A new breed of student prefers a new breed of sport, and they want to display their talents for all to see. While teachers may admire the dedication, balance, and plain old guts; students that hone skateboarding and mountain biking skills in the hallways, down the stairwells, and along railings are not to be encouraged. If a teacher is asked to coach the team, politely decline, claiming a prior commitment to coaching a more cerebral sport such as bowling or golf; *see Golf Team, Volunteer Labor.*

Y

YAPPERS

1. Constantly talking about nothing important, these colleagues fill up a great deal of air time in the staffroom. While even the most dim-witted student will eventually notice non-verbal signals to be quiet, the yapper colleague lacks this ability. A colleague may even be considered rude if not paying attention for the full twenty-minute soliloquy; *see Non-Verbal Communication, Politicos, Queen Bee, Watering Hole, Whine, Zero (a).*
2. A few colleagues like to blather on about their unending knowledge about teaching. This usually bears little connection to their ability to do the job. Principals and curriculum coordinators are frequent participants; *see Curriculum Coordinators, Job Interview (2), Laws of Bureaucracy (c), Principal (a), Zero (a).*

YARN When a teacher breaks up an altercation on an elementary playground; or attempts to understand the relationship intricacies of a group of early-adolescent girls; or attempts to ascertain the source of a teenager's vodka bottle at a school dance, a story that would rival a Joseph Conrad yarn will occur. Patiently waiting and probing for truth will do little good: the story will go on, and on, and on; *see Aides (b), Excuses, Judge and Jury, Untruthful Statement.*

YEARBOOK The academic year in review, this book highlights dances, hallway hijinks, and friends wrapped arm-in-arm. On occasion the editing is not as robust as it could be and images of senior students drinking beer at a party, or not-so-subtle hints about the sexual escapades of one of the more popular student couples is included. The teacher picture, featured year after year in the staff section, provides a visual archive of a slow but steady aging process; *see Beer, Graduation.*

YELLOW Knowledgeable about such things, only elementary teachers know, or care, that this is a primary color; *see Kaleidoscope.*

YOGI A yogi (not to be confused with the cartoon bear or baseball legend), may be contracted to deliver workshops on professional days for sessions on yoga and meditation. These training days are often accompanied by other professionally rewarding activities such as aroma therapy, herbal remedies, and vegan cooking; *see Knee-Deep Syndrome, Professional Development.*

Z

ZEALOT This term describes the majority of primary school teachers who save egg cartons, glass jars, old carpets, and cardboard packaging for use at work. They also frequently fill a room in their home with stored posters, flash cards, puzzles, prizes, and the like, all of which has been purchased with their own money; *see Altruism, Kindergarten Teacher, Pay Slip (2), Zero (b).*

ZEITGEIST Broadly translated from German this term refers to the spirit of the time. During much of the twentieth century the *zeitgeist* surrounding the importance of public education was positive support. The cause was considered noble philosophically, valid economically, and just socially. Alas, there are signs that the *zeitgeist* is altering in the initial decades of the current century, and not in a positive direction; *see Education (Public), Societal Expectations.*

ZERO This term applies to much activity in education and it is time for a little reader participation. It will not take long for a teacher or principal to add many more to the three that have been provided below as a starting point:

a) The number of times the staffroom will be quiet at recess or lunch; *see Yappers;*

b) The number of times the principal will allocate more resources to a project than a teacher needs; *see Budget, Zealot;*

c) The number of times any hard-earned knowledge of educational statistics will be useful; *see Median, Standard Deviation.*

ZIG-ZAG Certain moves are required so often and to such an extent that time should be provided in teacher training programs to develop the following:

a) an ability to navigate through crowded high school hallways, often requiring a skill level approaching that of a professional football running back;

b) an ability required to navigate through the never-ending insanity surrounding education reform, often needing a skill level approaching that of a professional politician; *see Flip Flops (2), Leading Edge, Innovation;*

c) an ability to throw a well-prepared lesson plan in the trash can in response to student apathy and adult interruptions and wing it for an hour; *see Lesson Plan (b/c/f).*

ZIPPER When positioned correctly this wardrobe necessity goes unnoticed; when not, the male teacher may face diminution of reputation. Male teachers should ensure that the zipper is in the up position at the beginning of every day. Required adjustments should be made in the male staff restroom or in an otherwise secure, private locale.

Printed in Canada